"Helen is a natural pathfinder. She brings a quality of luminescent clarity to the situation that is full of humor and vibrancy. She helped me focus on what really matters and find practical answers to my questions."

Siobhan Chandler,
PhD

"Helen's way of communicating is through coaching. In her program, she conveys her message like an artist, using her own unique palette that contains a blend of spirit, groundedness, and color. Her masterful strokes help her audience move to new depths of self-awareness that has them courageously reclaim their own beautiful landscape of life, full of wisdom and power, and step into action planting their seeds of vision, understanding, and progress with clarity and purpose. Her approach is dynamic, creative, compassionate, and simple at the same time."

Carlos Aranha
Internationally Renowned Artist
Painter, Sculptor, Installer, Performer, and Filmmaker
www.aranhaArt.com

"Working with Helen helped me establish a clear view of what is important to me and what I already have in my life. Our sessions left me with an inner sense of stability and calm, enabling me to have more powerful conversations in many areas of my life."

Heather W.
VP, Retail

"I approached coaching with a very clear idea of my strengths and weaknesses—Helen messed that all up. She deconstructs everything, scatters the pieces in front of you, and asks you to rebuild them. You see connections between pieces that you've never considered before. You also see a few pieces that you've been forcing together for years and wondering why they just didn't look right."

Randy Cameron
Illustrator

"Helen gets straight to the heart of the matter. She listens thoughtfully and helps to draw out my confidence and to focus on my natural strengths. Speaking with her, I feel supported, listened to, and understood. In a very short time, her insight and encouragement has helped me move forward with energy and excitement! You know those pivotal moments in your life that you realize changed everything that followed? For me, meeting Helen was one of those moments."

Daniella Rosales-Friedman
Dating Expert and Creator of The Inside Voice
www.theinsidevoice.net

"With a keen eye and an open heart, Helen is the one you want in your corner as you move through any of life's transformations. It is her special blend of holistic coaching and professional integrity that makes her program so effective. So whether you are making a career shift or pondering a complete life change, Helen can help you reach your greatest success and achieve your highest potential."

Karen Windsor
Windsor Communications

"Helen individualizes her coaching approach. She has challenged how I perceive my abilities and the possibilities for my life. I am empowered in knowing that every moment is an opportunity to work toward my goals."

Ann Lau
Editor

LITE Up™ YOUR WORK AND LIFE

Dear Maggie,
May this book
help your shine
your LITE!
Enjoy.

LITE Up

YOUR WORK and LIFE

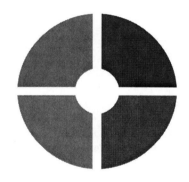

6 Essentials to Expressing
Your Full Potential

HELEN RODITIS

NEW YORK

LITE Up™ Your Work and Life
6 Essentials to Expressing Your Full Potential

ISBN 9781614482987 (paperback)
ISBN 9781614482994 (eBook)
Library of Congress Control Number: 2012936894

Morgan James Publishing
The Entrepreneurial Publisher
5 Penn Plaza, 23rd Floor, New York City, New York 10001
(212) 655-5470 office • (516) 908-4496 fax
www.MorganJamesPublishing.com

Thank You!

By purchasing this book, you are making a difference.
A percentage of the proceeds are being donated to
Habitat for Humanity.

A PURPOSEFUL LIFE

Nothing ever stays the same.
So why do you fight to keep it so?
Don't you know there is so much more?
A purposeful life is beyond money and fame.
Yes, you are destined to grow.
The universe knows what it has in store.
Follow your path without shame.
O, let the light of your heart glow
And cast its shine upon humanity's shore.

Helen Roditis

CONTENTS

PREFACE

The most important relationship you will ever have is the one you have with yourself. I realized this after many life transitions: I realized that at the center of my life was me. The time had come for me to take responsibility for my life and my work. As I began to work on my relationship with myself, I began to see how I was affecting the relationships around me, and how they had affected me. I began to see how I had made some of my choices. I came face to face with my light and darkness, my gifts and my self-limiting beliefs. And I continue to do so to this day.

Along the way, I have been fortunate to encounter the right people at the right time and place. These people have helped me open my heart, be authentic, and express my essence through a meaningful career and empowering relationships. Such encounters are available to all. Once you set an intention, you will begin to notice and meet the right people at the right time and place. Your choosing to read this book is no coincidence. You set an intention, and we too have connected for a reason.

The reason will become clear to you in time. Right now, I want to acknowledge you for being proactive and committed to your growth. While this book is not meant to heal all the world's woes, I hope for one thing: that it will help bring out your full potential as a leader who will make a positive difference, big or small, in this world.

Namaste,

Helen Roditis, ACC
Leadership Coach and Founder, essence coaching

P.S. For the curious-minded, *namaste* means, "When you see the light in me, and I see the light in you, we are ONE."

The Circle of LITE™

The Circle of LITE™

Most people yearn for more happiness. Each person pursues happiness differently. A great number of people look outside themselves for it. This book will have you look *inside* yourself for it. Your essence and innate gifts live inside you, waiting to be unleashed and expressed. Their expression is what manifests your full potential. Your full potential is what manifests positive change in our world. This is why it's so important that you embark on your own journey of personal development. I am honored that you have chosen to do so with me.

There are so many global issues that are calling for our collective attention and collaboration. When each of us taps into our full potential, however unique each full potential is, we can co-create a more balanced, prosperous, and healthy world. The world is full of good people who can and want to have a positive impact on our communities, starting with their own lives, no matter what stage of life they are in.

To help you journey within and bring out your full potential, I have created the Circle of LITE as a guide. The Circle of LITE is a coaching model based on my experiences living, working, and coaching hundreds of professionals and entrepreneurs. Essentially, the Circle of LITE is made up of six elements that represent your full potential in action (see Figure 1). Your self-esteem is at the core, because it is fundamental to your leadership, intellect, teamwork, and expression. Supporting these is balanced living, which includes work/life balance and stress management. These six elements are all interconnected; one will affect the other.

Figure 1. The Circle of LITE™. Developed by Helen Roditis, founder of essence coaching (www.essencecoaching.ca).

THE SIX ELEMENTS OF THE CIRCLE OF LITE

- *Self-esteem:* Reflects your sense of self-worth and level of confidence. People with high self-esteem have a high level of self-respect.
- *Leadership:* Your ability to bring out your best and the best in others while inspiring and empowering them to co-create a shared vision.
- *Intellect:* Your ability to maintain a healthy and open mind.
- *Teamwork:* Your ability to create and sustain unity within your team.
- *Expression:* Your ability to let the world see, hear, and experience you for who you are.
- *Balanced Living:* Your commitment to maintain a healthy body, mind, heart, and spirit through work/life balance and stress management practices.

In the upcoming pages, I will take you through each element in greater detail. You will also have an opportunity to self-assess where you are in each of these elements. You will notice the gaps you want to close by stepping into a new way of being and taking bold new action steps.

SETTING YOURSELF UP FOR SUCCESS

Before we begin our work together, I'd like us to clarify what it means to be living out of your *full potential.* Your full potential is about being who you are meant to be, fully expressing your passions, strengths, and innate gifts with purpose. Your full potential is your *wholeness* being expressed. Wholeness is unity with self, spirit, and our universe. Leading your work and life from an existence of wholeness will change the way you see the world around you, how you use your available resources (including money), and how you interact with the people around you.

This may sound inconceivable to you right now. So, as you work with the exercises throughout this book, I am going to ask you to imagine that you have all you need to be who you are meant to be. This will enable you to explore the possibilities with an open and positive mind, and connect with your authentic self.

You have all that you need to be your full potential.

WHO THIS BOOK IS FOR

This book is for employees, business owners, individuals in transition, and college/university students who want to gain more clarity about who they are and express their full potential in leading a purposeful life and career.

HOW TO USE THIS BOOK

While this book is divided into four sequential parts, I encourage you to read these parts in the order that feels right for you. The exercises within each part will help clarify your vision and who you are, provide you with practical insights, and move you towards a purposeful life and career. As in my live coaching sessions, my intention is to help bring out your own answers and innate wisdom. I am simply providing you with a framework within which you can do this. Keep in mind that the concepts throughout this book can be applied to your whole life. So, while I provide a framework you can apply at work, you can also apply this to your personal life, and vice versa.

As I love to share, you will find me sharing my own personal stories and insights based on my interactions with family, clients (anonymously and with permission), and others. These stories are set apart in italics.

DEFINING SUCCESS

Will living out of your full potential bring you success? What is success, anyhow? The answer depends on who you ask. Each one of us defines success differently. I remember being at a personal development seminar where the instructor asked us to put our hands up if we wanted to be successful. He asked us three times. Each time I kept my hand down. Why? I kept my hand down because I already felt successful. In my mind, I was thinking, "I *am* successful; I don't *want* to be successful." I was already experiencing success in the present moment, because I was happy with my action plan and progress and I was enjoying the journey. Certainly I had challenges. I embraced those too. My point is that *you* get to define what success means to you.

Go ahead; define what success means to you.

Success to me means: _____

_____

_____

_____.

Being clear on what success means to you is particularly important as we embark on our work together. You can redefine what it means to you as you move through the rest of the exercises throughout this book. With experience and self-reflection comes clarity. Your needs and wants may also change at each stage of life. Allow yourself to evolve and your definitions of success with it.

MAKING IT HAPPEN
Step 1: Admit

The first step to creating change is admitting to yourself that there is something you long for and would really enjoy having in your personal and professional life. More than that, having the courage to do something about it is essential.

You do have the power to evoke change. The question is, what is stopping you? What values and beliefs are behind the choices you are making right now? Are your current values and beliefs serving you? Do they reflect who you are and who you are becoming? As we grow and evolve, so do our values and beliefs. You will have an opportunity to identify, clarify, and work through your values and beliefs as we move through this book.

Be open to new information.

Step 2: Invest

Invest in yourself and your team, be it your team at work, your family, and/or your community. Your personal development requires your time and attention. Personal development resources come in varying formats and price points, from low-budget books to high-budget events such as retreats and conferences. Choose your resources wisely. Choose the ones that fit your financial budget and will help you create real change. This book is a great start and can be shared with your family and community.

Choose the resources that will help you create real change.

Step 3: Commit

You've taken the bull by the horns: you are investing in your personal and professional development. Your work is just beginning. Yes, it takes work. Creating positive change requires your effort and discipline to stay committed throughout the process of change. Partway through the coaching, around the three-month mark, I've seen coaching clients backtrack because they get scared or sabotage their success. They stick with what is comfortable and known, rather than explore and venture into the unknown. This is where coaches come in really handy. We help you clarify what you want, hold your focus, and cheer you on until you reach the finish line, that place where your vision lives and can become a reality!

Stay the course.

WHAT TO WATCH OUT FOR

How you approach the work we are about to embark on is as important as the work itself. It's easy to get sucked into feeling sorry for yourself, angry, or scared when you begin to take a closer look at your life and notice a gap between the life you are living now and the life you want to be living.

Applying a hearty and positive approach to your personal development will help you become who you are meant to be, get to where you want to go, and manifest the life you long for.

YOUR READINESS

As you embark on your transformational journey, you may find yourself in a bit of a catch-22. The very thing you are trying to rise above is the thing that is holding you back. When we forget that we are beings of potential, and that we have been beings of potential from the time we were conceived, our awareness of what is possible for us is blocked. That is, until someone reminds us. I am here to remind you that you are not broken. You are whole. Indeed, you are full of potential that you can manifest in your own unique way and pace. This potential lives inside of you.

Even though I am reminding you of your potential now, as you read through this book you will probably put it down here and there. In between the time you put it down and pick it up again, there will be moments when you will forget that you are a being of potential. And even as you read through this book and work on the exercises, there will be moments when you will forget who you really are. When you forget, your negative self-talk is taking over. This constant, negative self-talk will keep you stuck and stagnant, and distract you from being who you are meant to be—your full potential. I know you want to create positive change in your life. That is why you have picked up this book. So I want to prepare you now to watch out for your negative self-talk. We'll call your negative self-talk your *inner mocker*. You will learn to address and manage your inner mocker in the pages to come. You want to create positive change: you can, and you will.

So before we embark on your personal transformational journey, let's check in on how ready you are. Also, let's put in place a support system that will help you stay committed to your personal development.

EXERCISE: GETTING TO 100% COMMITMENT

Answer the following questions:

1. How committed are you to developing your full potential? Circle the answer that applies below.
   a. 100%
   b. < 100%
   c. Not at all

2. If you answered anything but 100% above, what would help you become 100% committed? Write your answer below.

3. Who can you buddy up with to do this personal development work, and who can hold you accountable? List a few people in your life you think would support you.

Accepting where you are right now on your transformational journey, having the confidence to develop the areas of your life that are calling for your attention, staying committed to your personal development, and making choices that will support your growth are the keys that will begin to release your full potential—your essence. I encourage you to stick with it. Every person who makes a 100-percent effort to be their full potential is one more person who is making a positive difference in our world. Lead by example. Be contagious!

PART I

Know and Love Your Core Self

Experiences come and go;
however, my love for myself is constant.

Louise L. Hay

CHAPTER ONE

Self-Esteem: At the Center of Your Work and Life

D o you ever wonder what is really behind the dysfunctional interactions we've all experienced in our professional and personal lives? For many, it comes down to self-esteem. Why do I say this? Because I have observed that the moment people start feeling good about themselves, they see others around them differently, and they begin to interact with them in a more positive way. So this tells me that when we work on our relationship with our self, all else falls into place to support our growth, the growth of our relationships, and the growth of our communities—locally and beyond.

What may or may not surprise you is that others may resist the positive changes in you and your relationship with them. We are creatures of habit, because the status quo creates an illusion of comfort, control, and possibly power. Change is scary to many. Change is like a mirror, reflecting who we are at any particular time in any particular situation. On the surface, our identity gets challenged and our strength of character gets tested. Yet deep within us lies our essence, the part of our being that is the core of who we are, no matter what. This is who *you* are, who you have been from the moment you were conceived: a being of potential. Most commonly, this is the part you've forgotten, as layers of childhood wounds and painful life experiences have blurred your vision. Over time, your life experiences may have distracted you from seeing and loving the being of potential you really are. Sometimes a traumatic life experience is what awakens your inner power, this dormant force that lies within you. When it does, harness this inner power, because it will help you manifest your full potential, your wholeness.

While I have experienced several traumas in my life, one experience haunted me more than any other: the death of my mother after her three-year battle with cancer. I was thirteen, which was a critical time for the development of my self-esteem and emotional well-being. I know now that for a long time I was emotionally lost. I viewed life as very short and feared death and disease. This may have explained some of my choices.

Needless to say, the choices I made in that state reinforced time after time that something had to change. So let's fast forward to years after my divorce. It's 2002, and I'm in a bar in Toronto with my Irish friends celebrating their friend's fifteen years in Canada. At this point I was entertaining the idea of changing my lifestyle. The parties, drinks, trips, money, and job were unfulfilling to me. Something was missing.

The bar was starting to get packed. We laughed over a few beers while standing and listening to the band. Suddenly, this man from out of the blue comes up behind me and slaps my heinie—and hard, I may add. Shocked, as this had never happened to me before, I turned around and asked point-blank, "What are you doing?" He was as shocked as I was and remained speechless. While he remained speechless, I decided in that moment that I was going to change my life. The slap in the heinie crystallized this. I immediately waved goodbye to my Irish friends and vanished into the night.

As I drove back home, I recalled a book I had read called Emotional Clearing. I remembered the author mentioning how shiatsu massage therapy can help clear emotional blocks that are getting in the way of living well. I could feel unprocessed emotions trapped in my body and knew I needed help releasing these healthily in a supportive environment. I got home and pulled out the yellow pages to find a shiatsu massage therapist. I picked the one whose logo and business name drew me in. I also noted he was a registered shiatsu therapist. Wondering whether he'd take me right away, I left him a voice message that very night. I was very serious about making life changes and felt empowered taking action.

Within days I was in his clinic, meeting him for the very first time. The minute I met him, I felt a very strong connection. He asked me why I had come to him, and I replied, "To clear my mother's death." I wasn't messing around. I meant business and got straight to the point. He asked a few more questions. He quickly understood what was trapped in my body. I worked with him for a year, and throughout that year, we built a very deep spiritual bond, like none other. This man helped me see my own gifts, opened my heart, and empowered me to live my dreams—so much so that I booked a three-month trip to Australia and New Zealand shortly after I left my corporate job, something I had always wanted to do.

During the early days of my trip to Australia, I received the worst news I could ever have received. I received an e-mail informing me that this man had just been diagnosed with terminal cancer. I had just gotten back from a hiking trip in Kakadu National Park in Northern Australia. From a high I went to a total loss.

As I sat there staring at the computer screen, I literally felt the floor beneath my feet disappear and spin uncontrollably. I completely lost my ground. This was the second young person under forty that I knew that was dying of cancer in the span of six months that year. I thought I was trapped in a nightmare. For days I cried uncontrollably, not knowing what to make of this. The news of his impending death struck a very deep chord within me. All the emotions, everything I had been clearing with him, were rushing to the surface through the news of his death. His death was the pinnacle of my emotional clearing. Was it a coincidence that I chose him out of all the shiatsu massage therapists in the yellow pages, or was this manifestation at its best and the universe working mysteriously?

His impending death had me wander out to the middle of a vacant park in Darwin, Northern Australia. My eyes were feeling tender from all the tears I had shed, and my stomach felt so raw. Tender and raw, with my hands to my stomach, kneeling on the grass with my head up to the big Australian blue sky, I asked, "What do you want from me?" I felt such intense despair.

In that long moment of silence, I began to feel the awakening of my dormant life force, my inner power. I could feel my life force, this powerful energy, moving from my solar plexus up to my heart and mind. This powerful energy that soared through me was my restored faith in spirit, accompanied by my conviction to live a different and better life than I had. In knowing him, I had gotten to know my whole self and my divine gifts. This manifestation, this deep spiritual connection I was blessed to experience with this man, was a sign that I had to put my innate gifts out there for the world and make a positive difference. I did not know how at the time; I just knew I had to start. I set that intention right then and there, and trusted that the answers would come just like this manifestation did.

Embrace all of your life experiences and life lessons. Your life experiences and life lessons reveal your innate gifts, strengths, talents, passions, and purpose. They also help clear the way to shed old self-limiting beliefs and patterns of behavior that no longer serve you or humanity. See your life experiences and life lessons for what they are: opportunities for personal growth. The time has come for you to awaken your inner power and reclaim your core self. Knowing and loving your essence is fundamental to the development and expression of your full potential. The more you know and love yourself, and allow yourself to live and learn, the more your essence will radiate. This is pivotal to manifesting your full potential, your wholeness.

EXERCISE: JEWELS IN THE MIDST

We can all remember a challenging time in our life. As challenging a time it may have been, there are pieces of our creative, resilient, and whole self to be discovered in it. There are jewels in the midst. These jewels are the guiding sparkles on our transformational path. Looking back on your life experiences, whether they were challenging, meaningful, passionate, or otherwise, what sparkling jewels do you see buried? Write them down in the space below. Distinguish the positive self-talk from the negative self-talk. The point of this exercise is to notice the jewels in the midst. Your negative chatter may intrude. Notice it and make note of it, because we'll work with it later in the book.

Significant life experience	What did you learn about life?	What did you learn about yourself?

Knowing and loving your core self has its own growth and development cycle. Wherever you are on this growth and development cycle is just right. We're all doing the best we can with what we know at the time. Each passing moment brings new awareness into your life. What you do with this new awareness is your choice. Here's the thing about making choices. Sometimes we will make a choice we think is right at the time. Months or years later, we feel or think differently about our choice. Some of us call it a "mistake." I prefer to call these "life lessons." Life lessons are empowering. They can help you get to know yourself intimately, and they can teach you how to love yourself unconditionally. With a positive attitude, life lessons can be self-esteem boosters.

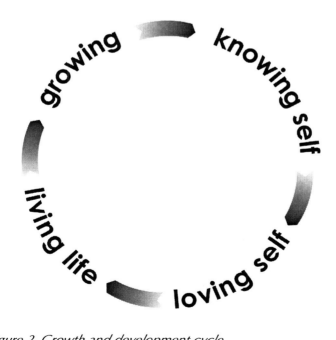

Figure 2. Growth and development cycle

UNDERSTANDING SELF-ESTEEM

Self-esteem is about stopping the judgments and healing old wounds of hurt and rejection. Your negative self-talk is profoundly affected by the negative core beliefs you have formulated based on past experiences. You may also notice that your negative self-talk is centered around certain areas of your life. Changing the way you perceive yourself (your thoughts and beliefs), and therefore how you feel about yourself, is possible. Rebuilding your self-esteem simply takes time and practice. Throughout your growth and development cycle, you will build, rebuild, and maintain your self-esteem.

Signs of high self-esteem

- You feel good about your core self.
- You believe you are a worthwhile person.
- You are happy to be who you are.
- You respect yourself.
- You make choices that support your well-being.
- When others reject you, you still feel good about yourself.
- You love yourself no matter what and are able to laugh at yourself when you experience "life lessons."

WHY IS IT SO IMPORTANT TO BUILD, REBUILD, AND MAINTAIN HIGH SELF-ESTEEM?

Self-esteem is central to your physical, mental, emotional, and spiritual growth. Neglecting your self-esteem can contribute to stress symptoms, cause you to enter into unhealthy relationships, negatively affect your performance, and simply bring you down.

Most of us have been conditioned to give and please others to the point of exhaustion. We say "yes" to others when we really mean "no," meaning we operate from a place of obligation rather than a place of joyful living. The irony is that this pattern ends up letting everyone down, perpetuating the cycle of lowered self-esteem.

By loving yourself, you are saying "yes" to you. And you matter. When you love yourself and give from this place, others can feel your authenticity. You are no good to anyone unless you are good to yourself.

WHAT CAUSES SELF-ESTEEM EROSION?

Over time, you, like everyone else, have been surrounded by external forces and social pressures that have distorted your view of your core self. Basing your self-esteem on volatile external forces and social pressures is harmful to your self-esteem. For example, you may run into a situation that has you feeling bad about yourself, such as getting laid off from work. You may then begin to condemn yourself. All that does is sap you of your vital energy and erode your self-esteem. By distinguishing the negative situation or event from your core self, you preserve your self-esteem. By viewing the situation as a "life lesson" separate from your self-worth, you not only preserve your self-esteem, you grow more confident and increase your self-esteem.[1]

HOW DO I STOP MY INCESSANT NEGATIVE SELF-TALK?

One way is to turn your attention away from your negative self-talk and listen to your inner core, your essence. Doing so will enable you to create and live a life you want and are meant to live. To ignore your negative self-talk altogether, you must first understand that your inner mocker is around to keep you stuck and stagnant. Sound simple so far? Ignoring your inner mocker is only half the challenge. You can move away from your inner mocker when you then begin to listen to your inner core and then take steps towards being your authentic self, or your essence.

Another way to stop your negative self-talk is to examine your inner mocker over time. When does your inner mocker show up? What does your inner mocker say? What have you made it mean? What's at risk? Keep asking yourself, and you will uncover the underlying self-limiting beliefs behind the self-defeating thoughts that come from your inner mocker.

A young professional came to see me not too long ago. She had met me a year prior at an event I had hosted and delivered. She proclaimed her readiness to do the personal development work that would have her feel more self-confident and demonstrate leadership in her new role at work. At this point in her coaching, we had come face to face with her fears in expressing who she was, a being of potential. Her familial values were in conflict with this desire, to the point where she had difficulty sharing her strengths, passions, and innate gifts with me. She viewed her homework as "boasting," whereas she had been taught to live a life of "humility." Kudos to her for being aware and sharing this with me. This helped me understand her inner conflict. Something brilliant came out of this sharing. We reviewed the purpose of the homework, which was simply for her to know herself. This was essential to her living out her full potential. I asked her to explore and discover this with me in our private sessions. How she presents it to the world is up to her. I acknowledged that she can express her full potential while honoring her values. This affirmation is helping her carry on with her personal development work.

Replace the self-limiting beliefs with affirming ones. This approach explores the rules your inner mocker has created and will have you follow. Facing your inner mocker head on can be an empowering process. You get to choose what you believe and what you say to yourself. Replacing your inner mocker with your inner champion is a choice available to you. Align the rest of your life with your new affirming beliefs and reinforce them with real, affirming experiences. We'll cover this topic in more detail in Part II of the book.

EXERCISE: SELF-ESTEEM ASSESSMENT

1. On a scale of 1 to 10, with 10 being the highest level, how would you rate your self-esteem?

2. What is contributing to your self-esteem, for better or worse?

3. What areas of your life are bringing you down?

4. What areas of your life are uplifting?

5. List the external forces playing havoc on your self-esteem. Remember, your core self is whole, beautiful, and full of potential, no matter what is happening around you.

6. What is your inner mocker saying?

7. What would your inner champion be saying?

8. What do you stand to gain by building up your self-esteem?

ACKNOWLEDGING YOUR STRENGTHS

We're going to step into the light. We're going to acknowledge your strengths. As mentioned earlier, we have been full of potential from the day we entered this world. What we do with it is our choice. I've said this before, and I'll say it again: for you to be doing this work right now tells me you are choosing to let your full potential, your essence, shine bright. So where do you go from here? Well, so far, you have an understanding of what self-esteem is; why it's important to build it, rebuild it, and maintain it; what your inner mocker is saying to you; and what your inner champion would say. Now I am going to ask you to do an exercise that will reveal the strengths you already share with your community. You are, in effect, going to listen to your inner core, or your essence, in doing this exercise, which is the opposite of listening to your inner mocker.

Here we go. I want you to think of a person you admire and aspire to be like. What about this person do you admire?

I've been asked this question, too. My father happens to be one of a handful I admire. He arrived in Canada in the late 1950s with only a few dollars in his pocket. Before I was born, he took on various sales jobs. When he gained enough experience and saved enough money, he started his own business. Ever since I can remember, I have watched him grow his small business with the help of friends, family, and loyal employees at the best of times and the worst of times. His constant optimism, positive attitude, and leadership during trying times are the traits in him I noticed from an early age. Watching him handle three recessions with such ease taught me that a person's intrinsic strengths are the intangible resources that are

available and accessible at any time, no matter what.
This knowing served my business and me during the
2008 financial downturn we experienced.

So take a moment and notice the very traits you admire in others and want to cultivate in yourself. These too are precious clues.

EXERCISE: MY STRENGTHS

1. Think of a person you admire and aspire to be like. Make a list of five to ten strengths you admire in that person, such as creativity, business smarts, compassion, and so on. Add on five other strengths you believe you have. Next I want you to rate yourself from 0 to 10, with 10 being the highest value, on each of these strengths. Next, rate the level of importance this strength plays in your life.

Strengths	Level of strength (0-10)	Level of importance (Low, Medium, or High)

2.   What are you noticing about yourself?

3.   Who are you?

Using the previous exercise, describe yourself by filling in the blanks below. Use your three most important strengths to describe yourself. You may find that the strengths that matter most to you require more development. This is natural.

I AM... _____ _____ _____

How do you feel now? Amazing, right? That's because you are amazing. Making a habit of remembering your strengths daily will support you even further in building your self-esteem to new heights.

ACKNOWLEDGING YOUR PASSIONS

People remember us by our passions. Have you ever met a colleague who shared their passion or an extracurricular activity they're passionate about with you? Ever notice how excited they get about it? Their passion is so memorable.

I recently reconnected with a former colleague of mine. What I remembered most about him was his creativity and love for acting. I had been thinking of taking some acting classes, and he immediately came to my mind. I even remembered going to see him in a play. The memory alone brought a smile to my face. When we met for coffee, he was pleasantly surprised when I recalled his acting days. Funny how he did not seem to think that his acting would be something I'd remember him by. This made me wonder, "How many of us go to our work or business, burying our passions?"

Let your passions shine! This is where your full potential lies. Your passions are for you to discover and share. When you share them, you are letting others get to know you. This is what connectedness is all about, getting to know each other.

EXERCISE: MY TOP FIVE PASSIONS

1. Take a moment to write down at least five passions.

2. To what extent are you living your passions? What next steps can you take to live your passions more fully?

3. What do your passions reveal about you? Complete the sentence below.

   I AM...

ACKNOWLEDGING YOUR INNATE GIFTS

Relationships are our mirrors. We discover parts of ourselves as we interact with the world around us. That being said, we are in relationship with our self too. Like a witness to your own life, you can see what innate gifts are showing up while you are in the experience of life. Your gifts differ from your strengths and passions in that they are a natural part of you, innate, and expressed effortlessly.

My sister, from a very young age, has had the gift of training animals. She was so young, yet she could naturally communicate with our cats and birds and get them to do what she asked them to. She trained our canary to kiss us on the lips while perched on our wrist! She trained our cats to take an elevator made of a cardboard box and string to the ground floor from the second floor. Within the last year, she has owned her gift. She owned it when she was ready and really—I mean really—saw it in herself. This was self-love in action. At fifty-one, she officially started her own dog-training business and volunteers her time to save animals from cruelty.

Owning our innate gift(s) is a self-loving act that multiplies and has a positive ripple effect. You can own your innate gift at any stage of life. How you use your innate gift is entirely up to you. You must first own it.

EXERCISE: OWNING MY INNATE GIFTS

1. List at least three gifts you know are special and come naturally to you. You may have noticed these yourself, or others may have pointed them out to you.

2. How can you use your innate gift(s)?

3. How would you like to use your innate gift(s)?

4. What do your innate gifts reveal about you? Complete the sentence below.

   I AM...

LOVING YOURSELF UNCONDITIONALLY

You are getting to know your core self. Now, how do you feel about your core self? Has your core self received all the love it needs? Well, let's take a look at what love is and where love comes from.

Simplistically, love is a pleasant emotion we feel, usually in our heart, when we are in a healthy relationship with our self and/or another person, or when we are doing something we are passionate about. Love connects us. At Journey into Healing, an event put on by the Chopra Center and delivered by Dr. David Simon, I learned that love is comforting when it meets our needs, such as our basic needs for attention, appreciation, acceptance, and affection. Love does not demand perfection. Most of us are still learning to practice unconditional love, a love that says, "I forgive you. I love you just the way you are right now, growing and evolving."

I remember delivering a sample coaching session, and the topic of forgiveness came up. I was asked, "How am I to forgive? How do you do this?" What a great question, and how timely it was. I had just learned to do this myself. One day I was feeling resentment towards a person in my life over something they had done years ago. I was aware of this and knew it would be healthier for me to let this go. As I struggled to do this, I looked at my cat's picture and admired his unconditional love for me. Pets have a tremendous capacity for unconditional love. They love us through thick and thin, through the ups and downs in our lives, through it all. This appreciation allowed me to be vulnerable and to notice my own imperfections. I realized that the very things I resented in this other person were the very things I resented in myself. What I was judging in the other person lived within me too. This was a humbling and freeing moment, one that allowed me to forgive myself and the other person.

To clarify, unconditional love does not mean you accept abuse. Setting healthy boundaries is a self-loving act. You can forgive, set healthy boundaries, and let go. One sure way of giving unconditional love to others is to learn to give it to yourself first. While there are several sources of love, you are your most reliable source of unconditional love.

Your core self is like a flower waiting to bloom. Your unconditional love is what will nurture your core self to become all it is meant to be. Your unconditional love will help heal the pain within that is getting in the way of your core self's full expression. You have already begun the healing process by picking up this book. You have gained some clarity around your strengths and who you are.

Likely there is room for more exploration and growth. With continued growth come mistakes. Learn from your mistakes. Make mistakes your allies rather than reasons to put yourself down. Continue to acknowledge, appreciate, accept, and pat yourself on the back wherever you are on your lifelong, transformational journey.

EXERCISE: SELF-LOVING ACTION STEPS

Actions you can take to support your growth and development:

1. Choose habits (practices) and behaviors (ways of being) that are self-loving, such as exercising with a smile.
2. Remove habits and behaviors that are not self-loving, such as addictions and negative interactions with others or yourself.
3. Make time for pleasant activities that nourish your life. This will help you see your life and progress with clarity and calmness.

Make a list of self-loving habits, behaviors, and/or activities you can add to your week. Also write down why this is important. This is what you are saying "yes" to.

Self-loving habits	Self-loving behaviors	Self-loving activities	Why this is important
Ex: Exercise 3 times a week	Follow-through	Join a tennis club	To stay healthy for the sake of pursuing my dreams

Write down a list of habits, behaviors, and/or activities you must stop. This is what you are saying "no" to.

Habits to STOP	Behaviors to STOP	Activities to STOP	Why this is important
Ex: Inactivity	Procrastina- tion	Watching too much TV	To stay healthy for the sake of pursuing my dreams

Often there are habits, behaviors, and activities we need to replace in order to live our values and create a life we want.

PART II

LITE Up™ Your Work

You, a person with a vision, are like a pebble in a stream,
moving ever outward to infinity, impacting all who
come into contact with the ripple.

Dr. Wayne W. Dyer

CHAPTER TWO

Leadership: Seeking Higher Ground

Anyone can be a leader. Leadership shows up day to day in how you live your whole life, in the impact you are having, and in the effort you put into your own personal development (not because you "have" to, but because you "want" to). After our basic needs are met, we have the space to grow into our full potential. How we use that space is up to each and every one of us. Leadership, put simply, is really about bringing out the best in yourself and others.

There are leaders who strive to excel so that they can make a positive difference in our communities and world at large. Their success allows them the freedom to fulfill their vision and their legacy. Money is one of their vehicles, a resource that comes with their success. Money, to them, is not the end but a means to the end. Their relationships are also resources they have available to assist them in fulfilling their legacy. And the more authentic and aligned they are with their vision, the more inspiring and contagious they become.

That being said, your title or status has very little to do with the quality of your leadership. A title and status are labels assigned that may not necessarily reflect who you are or your impact. Your leadership can show up in all sorts of areas of your life. While this part of the book is focused on leadership at work, your work can be in business, at home, or in your community. You can apply the concepts presented here to your whole life.

WHY LEADERSHIP MATTERS

Leadership matters because it is the driving force behind creation and its evolution. Whether you are creating a business, a partnership, a project, an event, or anything else, its success will depend on your capacity to envision your desired outcome as if it were happening right now, and your capacity to attract and retain relationships that will contribute to its creation. Notice I did not include any technical know-how as a major leadership competency. While technical know-how, such as software expertise or financial planning, is important, they can be provided by those you are in relationship with. All the technical know-how in the world will go nowhere without a shared vision and empowered relationships. As a leader, you can rely on the expertise of your team and listen to their ideas, opinions, and recommendations before making a decision. This shows great respect, engages your team, and creates better outcomes. While there is more to leadership than this, I will keep it simple and to the point.

WHOLE LEADERSHIP

Whole leadership is a leadership style that is made up of what I call the "middle path," "yin and yang," or "heart and mind." Striking a balance between heart and mind is what this entire world is calling for right now. We can see this by merely watching the news. Leadership is being called to evolve, yet again, to be more collaborative, empowering, and balanced. We are capable of such leadership. We each have personal development work to commit to for our collective full potential to be expressed. More and more we are seeing how interconnected we are; overpopulation, a finite amount of resources to go around, overconsumption, global financial chaos, global warming, inequalities, poverty, and illiteracy affect us all. As whole leaders, we can look at the big picture and understand how each one of us has a part to play in how the next generations will live on this miraculous planet, a planet I think, we sometimes take for granted.

Whole leadership is gender neutral, meaning that whether you are a man or a woman, you can lead with your heart and mind. You can be in relationship and a visionary.

Being a visionary: Leading with your mind

Have you ever asked yourself, "Why am I doing what I'm doing with my life and career?" I sure have. To this day, like peeling the layers of an onion, I am clarifying my own vision. While I wrestle with this at times, I know of inspiring leaders out there, who are successfully making a difference in their communities, who also wrestle with the same question on an ongoing basis. Will we ever get to a point where we can say, "This is it. I did it"? To get to "it," whatever "it" is for you, takes patience and the wisdom to listen to yourself, your heart, and passions. The good news is, once you peel one layer, there is less weight on the next layer. Layer after layer, we will get closer to "it." And while we are on this journey, there is joy to be had, because we are that much closer to being fully alive.

When an inspiring vision captures our hearts and minds, we are compelled to act and make it happen. When we do, not only do we see something we believe in take shape, we feel its power—the power that comes from connecting at a deep emotional level with others in a common purpose. For example, look at Earth Hour. I was listening to the 2012 Earth Hour video on YouTube and was amazed to hear how this cause initiative that started with one idea in one city has become a global movement with over 130 countries now participating. Billions of people around the world are connecting behind a common purpose for positive change: to save our environment. So because you are in the process of clarifying your own vision, let's take a look at where vision comes from and what inspires vision.

Aha! Here comes the connection. Vision comes from and is inspired by your essence and your innate gifts! You are capable of being a visionary. How do I know? You are reading this book. Like a muscle, you can develop your vision. The first step is getting to know your essence. The previous chapter began this process. Now what? Once you know your essence, you will know where to concentrate your energy. You will know because you will become aware of your purpose, your reason for being and doing, and the impact you will have on your business, local communities, and beyond. You will be able to figure out how to get from where you are now to where you are called to be. You will look for and connect to the information, people, and means you need to express your essence. You will learn to evolve as you chart a course along your path, bringing you closer and closer to your vision. Your vision will become clearer and clearer.

Organizations typically come to me for team development or high-performance coaching. Often the team is yearning for time to clarify the organization's vision. Teams want to know how they are contributing, to what they are contributing, and why. Just like individuals spend time exploring who they are and their purpose, so does a team.

Each one of us has a purpose. We own it when we do the work and stop making excuses. We express it when we decide to. Listen to your essence.

Your purposeful vision comes from and is inspired by your essence and innate gifts.

Leadership strengths of the mind

When we lead with our mind, we take into account all of the information, knowledge, wisdom, and expertise we have available to us to come up with a strategy and action plan. Vision inspires this plan, as does the team of people collaborating to make it happen.

- *Vision:* A mental image, thought, or concept created by our mind. Usually represents your values and ideal impact on your communities. This is the higher ground leaders pursue.
- *Strategy:* A plan designed to meet certain objectives and goals.

- *Action:* Execution of the strategy by a team of people.

*Imagine and co-create, keeping your eyes on your vision and
your feet on the ground.*

The leadership competencies of the heart feed the mind. The leadership competencies of the mind feed the heart. These competencies are interconnected and need to be for whole decisions to be made, decisions that have an overall positive impact on you, your team, your community, and beyond.

Being in relationship: Leading with your heart

Knowing and loving who you are at your core provides you with a strong foundation to build empowering relationships. Empowering relationships are based on authenticity, respect, and unity. When you show the world who you really are and share your vision, you will naturally draw to you the very people who respect you and your vision and will help you manifest your vision. Your vision is their vision. Like magnets, you will come together to create something extraordinary.

When each person gains awareness of their strengths, including those that need further development, self-managing becomes easier. Self-managing is important when working with others.

*I was caught by surprise when I was co-leading a team
coaching retreat. I had to self-manage and assert myself
to maintain the balance and harmony required to deliver
a successful retreat with my associate. Relationships are
complex. Despite all our training and development in
being effective leaders and team players, I witnessed our*

reactive impulses rise to the surface. The self-awareness I gained during my own leadership development helped me step back into the moment fully and notice the dynamic that was unfolding. I knew what tendency I needed to zap in the moment, and what leadership competency to step into that would best serve my clients, my associate, and me.

Gaining awareness of your reactive impulses is just as important as knowing your strengths. Such awareness will help you relate, communicate, collaborate, and make decisions in ways that honor your vision and what you stand for.

Leadership strengths of the heart

When we lead with our heart, we empower and engage others to collaborate with us and co-create win-win realities. We do this by communicating from the heart, with passion and empathy.

- *Empowerment:* Enabling another to become their full potential. Listening to others' ideas, opinions, and values is very empowering, as is helping them fully utilize their strengths, passions, and innate gifts.
- *Engagement:* Connecting with others at an emotional level. Getting curious about others, asking powerful questions, and listening to them attentively allows you to get to know them and connect with them.
- *Empathy:* The ability to understand others and feel for them. When you learn to process your own emotions and allow yourself to be vulnerable, you are that much more able to empathize with others. You become more comfortable listening to others when they are vulnerable

and sharing their feelings, and more open to exploring their feelings for the sake of understanding them.

Listen and relate from your heart.

What's love got to do with it?

In May of 2011, I exhibited at the Toronto Entrepreneurs Conference, where I heard Robert Herjavec, star of the CBC TV show Dragons' Den, speak. While he attributes his success to many things, he is very aware and openly admits that his heart was and continues to be in his business. Throughout the entire hour he spoke, he captivated us with his humor, humanity, and entrepreneurial wisdom. The one piece of advice he gave us that stuck with me was to follow our heart: if we believe in what we offer, then we can find a way to sell it. Whether you are an employee or an entrepreneur, passion sells.

I believe that passion does sell when it is communicated in a way that resonates with the right audience. I have to chuckle now, because I occasionally do watch Dragons' Den on CBC (similar to Shark Tank on ABC). These shows give entrepreneurs the opportunity to present their business proposal to a handful of savvy investors, Robert Herjavec being one of them and Kevin O'Leary being another. Not too long ago, there was a group of life coaches on the show selling "bucket list" coaching and activities via an Internet community, or something like that. Kevin O'Leary squashed this "fluffy" coaching business proposal in no time. What happened there?

What was missing from this presentation? Was it passion or something else? I wondered.

My guess is that a Kevin O'Leary–type needs us to "show him the money" for his resistance to "fluff" to evaporate, particularly when it comes to business. Fluff has come up in my conversations with a couple of executives throughout my coaching career. Some resist fluff. Their resistance made me ask, what is fluff? I even looked it up in the web dictionary. Fluff is defined as something soft. I may be taking a leap here, but I think that for some, following one's heart in business is considered fluff.

As a certified coach, I can assure you that fluff is what makes a leader great! That's right. Relating to, empathizing, mentoring, coaching, inspiring, motivating, co-creating with, and leading people have a lot to do with our heart. According to a new breed of biologists and neuroscientists, we have five different neural structures, or brains, within us. Four are in our head. The fifth brain lies in our heart. This head-heart dialogue that happens through direct neural connections affects our awareness and our ability to empathize and relate. A healthy dialogue between head and heart is what enables us to rise above constraints and limitations, tap into our full potential, and take right action.[2] Take the heart away, and what do you have? You have half a leader and half a team. A whole leader and a high-performing team integrate heart and mind.

So the next time you doubt your heart's place in business, think again, and let your loving feelings flow to your creative and resourceful mind.

Communication connects both heart and mind

Communication is the bridge between your heart and mind, and your world and you. Your heart will feed your mind, and your mind will feed your heart. As long as your mind works on its own, your leadership is half-informed and could be the cause of negative consequences to the world around you, a world that is

Figure 3. Heart and mind communication

interconnected. On the other hand, your heart working with your mind will produce practical, realistic, and applicable action steps that will manifest your vision while considering the long-term impact on our interconnected world. Heart and mind need each other. This is what makes us whole.

While whole leadership is an empowering and collaborative model, the ultimate decision making and responsibility that comes with it rests with you. There will be times when your leadership will feel less than whole, such as when you move your focus away from your vision, or feel disconnected within, and communicate decisions from this place. There will be times when you will be called to make some decisions and your heart may feel heavy in the process. However, these tough decisions may very well be the decisions that need to be made relative to the big picture. Communicating these in the face of adversity takes guts. In Part IV, we will work on processing both light and heavy emotions.

To stay whole as a leader, remember who you are daily; let your vision be a reflection of who you are; bring your whole heart and mind into your leadership; and keep your eyes on your vision. In other words, be your whole, authentic self. When we develop into whole leaders, we begin to tap into our full potential and bring out others' full potential. We co-create win-win realities. Imagine what would be possible if each person on this planet were empowered to express their full potential.

Notice your impact.

LEADERSHIP UNDER STRESS

Life is full of stressors, in our personal and professional life.

A few years ago stress had gotten the better of me. My stress level was off the chart. I was grieving, I had left my corporate job, and I had suffered a physical injury falling off a horse — all in the same year. Yes, it was a rough year, and my physical, mental, and emotional well-being paid the price, until I joined the Mindful Based Stress Reduction program, developed by Jon Kabat-Zinn and delivered at a nearby health clinic. This program helped

me reverse the cumulative negative effects of mismanaged
stress on my body and mind.

In this program, I learned that I had been caught up in reacting to stress. Let me explain. Before we even react to stress, the first thing that happens is a negative thought. That negative thought leads to more negative thoughts. All those negative thoughts lead to feelings of helplessness, powerlessness, anxiety, and fear. Life feels out of control, and we react. Our reactions can show up as controlling and protective behaviors; irritability; lack of focus; and illness, including depression.

stressor > negative thoughts > negative feelings > stress reaction

The pattern can go on and on and have a cumulative negative effect on our physical, mental, emotional, and spiritual well-being. This pattern can lead to high absenteeism, reduced productivity, and lower morale at work, perpetuating the reactive pattern in our whole life. Unless managed, stress builds up.

The good news is that we can learn to dance with stressors. The first step is to accept that life is filled with stressors, including change. So often we get caught up in life's circumstances, sometimes crisis. Being biologically set up to fight or flee when you perceive "danger," you may find yourself doing just that in times of stress. There is another way. You can respond to your stress rather than react to it. A great grounding force is your vision. Yes, the vision you have for your whole life. We've come full circle, haven't we? I know, not all you wish for is necessarily going to happen, and some things are beyond your control. I agree. However, all your choices are within your control. Whatever comes your way, you can choose how you will respond to it. The clearer you are about your vision, the more empowering your choices will be, and the more likely you are to turn your vision into reality.

stressor > vision/coping practices > commitment > responsive action

Sometimes life unfolding the way it does gives us the nudge we need to reset our vision. That is your choice. Keep in mind that vision alone may not have the staying power you need to deal with your stressors. Adding stress management practices to your daily activities will also help you cope and commit to respond healthily to your stressors consistently. We will go over some stress management practices in Part III.

EXERCISE: MY LEADERSHIP

1. What is your vision for your work? Write down what you would ideally like to see come out of your work five or more years from now. This includes your entrepreneurial, organizational, project, charitable, or any other work.

2. What aspects of your vision reflect who you are? Explain how.

3. Which of your values (what you care most about) does your vision honor?

4. How does your current job/role align with your vision?

5. How does your current lifestyle align with your vision?

6. What would you need to do to align your current job/role and lifestyle with your vision?

7. Of the relationships you have now, which are of service to your vision?

8. What other relationships do you need to develop in service of your vision?

9. What stressors are distracting you from your vision?

10. What could you do differently to respond healthily to your current stressors?

11. Describe your leadership style on most days. Circle the most appropriate answer.
    a. I am all heart.
    b. I am all mind.
    c. I am both heart and mind.

12. What else would you like to acknowledge about your leadership?

13. How satisfied are you with your communication?

14. What could you do to improve your communication?

15. How can you stretch your leadership? List the heart and mind competencies you would like to integrate into your leadership style.

16. Describe the impact your leadership is having on your work, life, and community.

CHAPTER THREE

Intellect:
Minding Your Mind

Different people have different levels of interest in learning, or gaining knowledge. Access to education is also different around the world. Those of us who can read, understand, and appreciate this are very fortunate. We can choose to learn as much as we want by reading. That being said, there are a variety of ways in which we acquire knowledge and wisdom.

GAINING KNOWLEDGE

Knowledge can be acquired through education or experience (be it visual, auditory, tactile, or otherwise). Facts and information gathered contribute to our knowledge base. The vast amount of facts and information out there is incredible. How do we know that all we know is enough to make a sound decision? Ever find yourself looking at a situation from another perspective, once you discover new information? How do we even know that a fact is a fact? We've all heard about scientific tests that contradict one another over time. A particular unknown variable could make a huge difference to the outcome of any scientific experiment. The real truth can be elusive, because we don't know what we don't know. This is a humbling admission.

Being aware that we may only have partial information allows us to be open to other possibilities. This can work in your favor, particularly when you have formulated certain limiting beliefs based on certain repeated experiences. Your full potential depends on your openness to new information and experiences. Ever notice how the most admirable and effective leaders are the most humble? They are always open to new information and ideas; because they are humble, they know that they don't know what they don't know. Being open to new information demonstrates their exceptional listening and relationship skills. Some of this information comes from their team. When their team feels heard, their team also feels respected. Listening to and understanding others is an incredibly powerful way to acknowledge them. Such reciprocation is the foundation of co-creation at its best; there is flow and synergy; new ways of seeing, thinking, and creating are embraced.

GAINING WISDOM

Wisdom is gained in every life experience. You gain wisdom when you apply your knowledge in real life, and when real life reveals new insights for you to apply. Wisdom is different from intelligence. Intelligence is based on how much and how well you know what you know. Wisdom is based on what you do with the knowledge you have.

Knowledge and wisdom assist your imagination.

YOUR MIND

How you use your mind is pivotal to developing your full potential. Your mind is the source and filing center of your knowledge, thoughts, perceptions, memories, emotions, will, and imagination. Your mind is where you have conversations with yourself about yourself, your life, and community. And these conversations can either boost you or bring you down. Whatever you feed your mind will show up in your leadership and the impact you will have on those around you.

Believing in yourself

So often we race through our day and forget to stop and listen to our higher self. So often we let distractions and self-defeating thoughts take over. Thoughts like:

- I'll be happy when…(a certain condition is met).
- Making money doing what I love is impossible.
- I'm a failure.

Do you notice how extreme these thoughts are? Such negative self-talk is coming from your inner mocker. It's not uncommon for your inner mocker to go to extremes. Your inner mocker will make absolute assumptions, fantasize, generalize, label, dwell on the negative, compare, blame, and personalize. All for the sake of keeping you distracted and stuck. And you know when your inner mocker is around, because your inner mocker's company is unpleasant.

The greatest roadblock to a client's full potential is his or her mind. Time and time again, I have encountered clients who stop their progress with their resistance. I let them know that this is a natural occurrence in the coaching process, and we set up a warning system. Usually I can see them slipping back. With a warning system, the responsibility for identifying such an occurrence falls on both of us. We call it, and we deal with it. Usually there is some fear or negative self-limiting belief behind the slipping. We explore it and move through it.

Ninety percent of our decisions are made by our subconscious mind. So be aware of this tendency, and question yourself when you start resisting change. Your resistance could be a positive sign, a sign to challenge yourself and stretch you into a new way of life.

How you use your mind

Your mind is made up of two parts, the conscious and subconscious. The conscious part of your mind is objective and rational. The subconscious part of your mind is creative and intuitive. Your habitual thinking lives in your conscious mind and makes its way into the depth of your subconscious mind. Once your subconscious mind accepts your habitual thoughts, it goes on autopilot to manifest those thoughts.[3] The amount of time it takes to manifest those thoughts can vary. This gives you an opportunity to assess whether your habitual thinking is serving your higher good. You can choose to continue your habitual thinking, or to change it. To change it, you need to examine the beliefs behind your habitual thinking. This is important, because it takes more than a positive thought or affirmation to alter the course of your life. You need to believe in your positive thoughts; they need to be supported by affirming beliefs you truly possess within you.

Shortly after my shiatsu therapist had passed away, I channeled my despair into advocacy. I, again, picked up the yellow pages (this directory has played a mystical role in my life—I can laugh about it now!) to look for an advocacy group I could join to help change the way young people with a history of cancer are treated in their doctor's office. I was warmly welcomed to join a high-profile forum where several not-for-profit organizations, pharmaceutical companies, health professionals, cancer survivors, and caregivers came together. When I went there to share my observations on the cancer-care system in Ontario, Canada, I also received new information that radically altered my own beliefs. As I listened to one reputable oncologist after another present the statistics and the causes of the various types of cancers, it became very clear to me that "how" I live my life, or my "lifestyle," has more to do with cancer than genetics. Many cancers are preventable. They are especially preventable when caught early. The relief I felt from hearing this from such credible people completely changed how I felt in my own body. I felt renewed. In that moment, I instantly reversed years of negative habitual thinking around my own health.

The point I am trying to make here is that new information from sources we trust can radically and quickly alter our habitual conscious thinking down to our very core. These are, as Oprah Winfrey would say, "aha! moments."

EXERCISE: MASTERING MY MIND

1. How do you nurture your mind?

2. What do you do to declutter your mind?

3. How often does your inner mocker interfere with your decision making?

4. What else would you want to learn or experience in life?

5. How hungry are you for this new learning or experience?

6. What about it has you so interested in it?

MANAGING YOUR INNER MOCKER

First things first: let's get you out of your own way. How do you get around your inner mocker? How do you go from extreme, self-defeating thoughts to a clear and reasonable self-knowing?

As we saw in Part I, we can manage our inner mocker in two ways: examining our inner mocker over time, and shifting our attention away from our inner mocker in order to listen to our essence.

Notice when your inner mocker comes around and how you feel when it does. When does your inner mocker show up? What does your inner mocker say? What have you made it mean? What's at risk? Keep asking yourself, and you will uncover the underlying, self-limiting belief behind the self-defeating thoughts that come from your inner mocker. Replace the self-limiting beliefs with affirming ones. Align the rest of your life with your new, affirming beliefs so that you can reinforce them with real, affirming experiences.

Listening to your inner core, your essence, takes commitment: a commitment that comes from believing in yourself. "How can this be?" you may ask. See, the fact that you are working with this book is evidence that you do believe in yourself. You are tapping into your core, your essence that is your whole and beautiful self, this very moment. Now, take five deep breaths and relax. Let your mind listen to your essence. Feel the nudge from your essence deep within you, calling you forward, calling you to be brave, calling you to take an even bolder step and let your essence shine bright. Can you feel the nudge? Where do you feel the nudge? Now, listen to the wise words coming from this place within you. What do you hear? Take a moment and listen. Now start journaling what you felt and heard.

Know that you can tap into your inner core, your essence, at any time. Go on and test out your new ways of being. Make note of your successes. This will reaffirm your new ways of being.

EXERCISE: MANAGING MY INNER MOCKER

Over the next week, take note of situations that bring out your negative self-talk and feelings. Notice your old way of being that is behind your core belief and driving your inner mocker. The following week, step into a new way of being to replace your old way of being

Situation (fact)	Negative self-talk	Feeling/ core belief	Old way of being	New way of being
Ex: The work I did on a project was abandoned.	"How desperate of me to take this on!"	Humiliated, not good enough	I have to prove myself.	I invest my time and talent wisely.

CHAPTER FOUR

Teamwork:
Sustaining Unity

A lot of what we do day-to-day requires that we communicate and collaborate with others. Who we surround ourselves with and the dynamic that gets played out usually reflect where we are in terms of our own growth and development. Every relationship is a mirror, and it is often fertile ground for transforming unfinished business or unresolved emotions from past relationships. To some employees, bosses are reminders of someone from their past, and what gets played out at work is an old familiar pattern.[4] Every encounter is an opportunity to stretch beyond our comfort level and to replace old, self-limiting beliefs. The cycle of growth, as mentioned earlier, carries on in every living moment and experience we have.

The more you stretch beyond your comfort level, the more you get to know yourself and clarify your vision. This is essential to teamwork. For a team to prosper, the team players must sustain unity. For the team to sustain unity, each team player needs to have a good idea of who they are, their strengths, their passions, what they stand for, what matters most to them, and how they would like to contribute. Only then can each team player communicate authentically with their teammates, discover their common ground, and turn their collective vision into reality.

SUSTAINING UNITY

Sustaining unity is about keeping our eyes on the big picture for the sake of the whole (not the individual parts). Sounds simple enough. Yet when you have many individuals on a team, many teams in an organization, many organizations in a community, many communities in a country, and many countries in the world, you can see how far from simple it is to sustain unity. Each will have different points of view, beliefs, values, ideas, and conflicting interests, and these may change over time. While you may feel unity within your team now, keep in mind that as the team and its environment evolve, so will the team. For example, during uncertain economic times, team members may begin to feel insecure about their jobs and feel threatened by one another. Conflict is known to escalate during uncertain times.

The reality is that conflict arises for a variety of reasons at all times. In organizational teams, conflict is a reflection that individual team members are out of alignment with themselves, or their team. These individuals may need to revisit who they are being and wanting to become, and how they can and want to contribute. Or the team needs to revisit or clarify their collective vision together. This process is very dynamic. Team members who once shared the collective vision may no longer feel in alignment with it because they have evolved and need to move on. Other times, conflict arises because our old self-limiting beliefs are driving the behaviors that are getting in the way of expressing our full potential, individually or collectively. Conflicts are opportunities to notice how you are getting in your own way and your team's. They also can reflect how much you have grown or need to grow. Remarkably, opposing ideas that present themselves at times of conflict can be the very seeds of creativity and innovation. The more diverse the team, the more likely the team will have varied and opposing ideas that can be converted into creative and innovative solutions. Teams just need to learn how to do this respectfully. When viewed in this light, conflict can nurture our leadership and team development.

So how do we sustain unity? Let's keep it simple and look at how you can sustain unity in a small team to start.

Steps you can take to sustain unity in a team:

- Observe and notice what is.
- Choose a facilitator (internal or external).
- Name the problem, challenge, or obstacle (not the symptoms). Get to the core issue(s). If you're not sure whether you've identified a symptom or the core problem, keep asking your team, "What is behind this?" Eventually you will get to the core problem.
- Have an open discussion about the core issue(s) and share each of your perspectives without blame.
- Commit to resolving the issue(s) together.
- Seek the higher ground—your common vision, one that inspires each of you.
- Brainstorm ideas to resolve the core issue(s).
- Listen to each other.

- Allow each of your strengths, passions, and gifts to inform your next steps.
- Respect each other's ideas and opinions.
- See what you come up with.
- Agree on a course of action.
- Take action!

Then what?

Monitor your success. You may need to go over the steps above more than once. You may also need to adjust your course of action. Be patient with yourselves and each other.

What to watch out for:

- You may have a team member who is out of alignment with himself or herself. In other words, this person could be in the wrong career, have work/life balance challenges, or have other personal issues beyond the scope of team coaching. One-on-one coaching or counseling may be beneficial here.
- Some team members may discover that they are not and will not be in alignment with your team, period. What you have here are deal breakers. Let each other go.
- You may have a team member who has the potential to be in alignment but whose attitude or mental-health issues need to be addressed in private.
- Individuals or teams sometimes get in their own way or sabotage their potential. This has a lot to do with their level of self-esteem and self-awareness. Again, one-on-one coaching may be beneficial here.

- You may have team members who are not clicking with one another or are in conflict due to unmet needs. Offering coaching training to managers and directors can help them build more positive relationships with their team members.
- You may need to examine the underlying causes of on-the-job stress from excessive pressure, workload, and overtime to avoid burning out your team.

What you can do:

- Offer one-on-one coaching to address any personal issues your team member may be facing.
- Agree in advance how you will handle such situations with your team.
- Be transparent—that is, do not have side chats with other team members about a "team" issue. Discuss "team" issues with the whole team.
- Sometimes the best solution is to help a team member move on.
- Identify signs of "sabotage" without blaming any one person. Move your team's focus onto its vision and further developing its strengths.
- Offer leadership and team development programs.
- Offer wellness programs.

There is wisdom in every situation. When we move away from blame to observe the natural unfolding of our relationships without attachment or judgment, we are allowing this wisdom to guide us. Every feeling, expression, or behavior within your relationships is a message for you to notice it, listen to it, and explore its meaning and significance. By exploring all that is arising, the answer will be revealed. When we see and accept the truth in this wisdom, we can take responsibility for ourselves and our team.

In the last year, I have been working with a creative team, one filled with three different generations. Moving a team from where they are to where they want to be can take six to twelve months of monthly sessions and mini-retreats. The individuals who make up the whole are in different places in their growth and have varying levels of self-awareness. As a coach, I notice what shows up over time and have candid discussions with the team about it. The coaching program evolves naturally, so that we can get to the core issues of the team and bring out its best. In this case, we are shifting the coaching to one-on-one leadership coaching, because what is showing up in the team is what is showing up in its leadership.

Each of you, and your teams, will have a ripple effect on others. Strong leaders will help create unity, and unity will help create strong leadership. You can create unity with an inspiring common vision and whole leadership: leadership that brings out team members' full potential by giving them opportunities to fully express their strengths, passions, and who they are.

MORE COMPANIES ARE EMBRACING COACHING

Career, leadership, and team coaching are gaining popularity. Organizations are in the midst of implementing, or already have in place, internal and external coaching programs for middle managers and above. It used to be that only high-potentials or executives would have access to coaching. Today, companies are beginning to see the value in hiring coaches and making them available to middle management as well. This is particularly the case in larger, progressive organizations that want to retain good employees and accommodate their lifestyle by helping them map out their career path over the long term. These companies realize that there are only so many top spots, and that their employees need to feel valued regardless of their title. Career mapping has less to do with the title employees carry on their business card and more to do with them being in the right career and work environment, fully utilizing their unique strengths, passions, and innate gifts, and being fairly compensated. There will always be those who strive to move into a company's top spots. When these high achievers find themselves unable to move upward at their current employer, they will try to find another employer who will satisfy their desire or start their own business. So identifying high-potentials and satisfying their hunger for upward mobility is still necessary. This process usually reveals a company's leadership culture.

What is coaching?

Let me start by saying that coaching is not advice giving, telling someone what to do, or therapy. Coaching is about bringing out the best in people, empowering them to be all that they can and want to be, and helping them get there. Certified coaches do this by tapping into their clients' own answers, their innate wisdom.

Benefits of coaching programs

While organizations reap benefits from coaching programs, so do employees. Helping people map their careers, deal with work/life stressors, work more effectively in teams, and lead their teams is being socially responsible.

Benefits to employer

- Increased productivity
- Lowered disability claims
- Improved relationships
- Constructive communications
- Unity
- Higher engagement and retention rates
- Bottom-line growth
- Preparedness for succession planning
- Enhanced employer brand

Benefits to employee

- Greater self-awareness
- Alignment with self
- Renewed optimism
- Emotional relief/support
- More energy
- Enhanced relationships
- More confidence
- Higher performance
- Greater job/life satisfaction

Coaching programs are part of the solution. Together with other resources, such as Employee Assistance Programs, health insurance benefits, and other perks, a complete solution is possible.

Is everyone coachable?

Not everyone is coachable. To be coachable, clients must be open, ready, and committed to the process. Anyone who is hungry for positive change, who wants reinforcement to keep their momentum going in creating their desired changes, and who demonstrates follow-through is coachable. Athletes have coaches. Why not you?

Coaching for potential

Coaching for potential is about stretching employees to fully utilize their gifts, talents, and passions in fitting roles. When employees are coached for potential, they produce exceptional work. Magic happens when an employer taps into their employee's potential.

A prerequisite to coaching for potential is career coaching, or helping employees know who they are, their interests, their values, their strengths, and their passions. Many young employees, right out of university, begin their career only to find out they chose a career that doesn't match who they are. This doesn't surprise me one bit. There is a discovery and exploration phase in landing a career that fits. And with time, values, interests, and passions shift. So it is not unusual for an employee— or business owner, for that matter—to want to change careers more than once in their lifetime. In light of the above, coaching for potential is an ongoing process that calls for patience, compassion, and empowerment.

Three steps a team leader can take to coach for potential:

- Watch for signs of a career misfit in your team, such as:
  - ✓ Employee tardiness
  - ✓ High absenteeism
  - ✓ Lack of interest, enthusiasm, or inattentiveness

- Train managers to coach their team and apply empowering coaching skills that will bring out their team's full potential.
- Offer external, one-on-one career coaching to employees.

Keep in mind that what may appear as a career misfit may be a sign of something else, such as work/life imbalance or other personal issues. Employees have a whole life outside of work with additional stressors. While they may not speak of such stressors, they do come to work with them on their mind.

CREATING A POSITIVE WORK ENVIRONMENT

When we think of career fit, how much consideration do we give to work-environment fit? In the short term, it may make sense to steer clear of work environments that are a "misfit." In the long run, it is in everyone's best interest to create a positive work environment, starting at the top of the organization. This would help alleviate much of the job-related stress employees experience currently. Why lose out on an employee who is in the right career but in the wrong work environment? Wouldn't it be more productive to learn how to foster a positive work environment and retain the talent within it as best as possible?

Most work environments face the same issues, such as poor communication and destructive interactions. This can explain some of the turnover experienced in companies. Really, many issues can be resolved with leadership and team development programs that are designed to bring out every employee's full potential. It boils down to making such programs available.

Every individual on a team has something unique to offer to the team in realizing its vision. The more each individual on the team knows who they are and how they can and want to contribute, and the more they develop into whole leaders, the more synergistic the team. With synergy comes high performance.

Focus your attention on developing your team's strengths.
Destructive interactions will naturally drop off.

EXERCISE: MY TEAM

1. How united is your team? Circle the most appropriate answer below.
   a. We are very united.
   b. We are a little united.
   c. We are not at all united.

2. What seems to be in the way of your team pulling together?

3. What is polluting your team environment?

4. What do you notice is behind the team pollutants?

5. What would be possible for your team were it 100% united?

6. What heart-and-mind leadership competencies does your team need to stretch into more?

7. What else does your team need to get to 100% unity?

CHAPTER FIVE

Expressing Who You Are: The Key to Feeling Connected

hile it takes courage to clear the way and finally see
yourself for who you are, it takes even more courage
to let the world see you, hear you, and experience you for who
you are. Yet being seen, heard, and experienced as you truly are
is a deep yearning within you, as it is in all of us. When you
allow others to experience you as you are, you allow for a
deeper connection with the people around you to happen. This
enriches their life and yours. In the process, you gain an even
deeper connection with yourself.

Like the rest of us, your fears can be blocking the expression
of your full potential. As a certified coach, I have done a lot of
personal development work on myself, and I continue to go
deeper and deeper. There is layer upon layer of fears and self-
limiting beliefs to clear. On the other side of it, a state of
euphoria awaits you. Moving past our fears is exhilarating.
Another reality exists past the fear. And you can create this
exhilarating reality for yourself.

Many times I notice people are avoiding the personal development work because they are afraid of facing their fears and what they might discover about themselves. They are afraid of change, the possibility of failure and all that comes with it. They are afraid to go for the very thing that they really want: to be and express who they are.

My own journey has been bumpy and filled with fear. When I first started out on my personal growth journey, it was suggested I remind myself of how loved I am with a daily affirmation. I had no idea how much emotion this would evoke in me. I remember going back to my meditation group overwhelmed. This loving feeling had me feeling "out of control" because suddenly anything was possible; there was room for expansion and I had no idea what I'd fill this room with. After repeating this daily affirmation to myself for days and months on end, my resistance broke down and I started to feel good; I started to really feel the love in and around me. This opened my eyes. I felt I had come to a crossroads. I could carry on playing small, or fill this expansive room with my essence. I chose to stop playing small and start expanding. Playing small did not feel good; it simply was familiar and gave me a false sense of power and control over my life. Consistently reminding myself that I am loved unconditionally gave me the courage to take baby steps and risk making mistakes in developing and expressing my own full potential. Once I let go of my fear and let the love in, there was no turning back. I had a destination to get to: my full potential.

Choose unconditional love and let go of unnecessary and paralyzing fear. This will help you step into a world filled with an abundance of possibilities, rather than a world filled with limitations. You can choose which of your gifts and talents you will share, how and when you will share them, and with whom you will share them. Your choices will largely be influenced by your vision: a reflection of your essence, values, and purpose.

The time has come for you to express who you are.
The world is ready for you.

EXERCISE: EXPRESSING MYSELF

1. How are you expressing yourself to others now (i.e., verbally, in writing, artistically)?

2. Imagine you are giving a speech. What would be your key message?

3. What impact would you like your message to have?

4. How else would you like to express yourself?

5. What's stopping you?

PART III

LITE Up™ Your Life

Become a conscious vessel for the life force
that is always flowing through you.

Christiane Northrup, M.D.

CHAPTER SIX

Balanced Living: What You Need to Thrive

Fundamental to the development and expression of your full potential is balance. We all strive to be in balance on a daily basis. The reality is that life is full of stressors. The most prevalent life stressors are on-the-job stress and financial pressures. These stressors are compounded during an economic crisis. And they are interconnected with other parts of your life, such as your health, family relations, social engagements, recreational activities, etc.

The more you push these stressors under the rug and keep going and going, the more likely you will crash and burn. You are no different than a battery. You only have so much energy to give without replenishing. The key is to replenish and revitalize your energy with healthy daily habits and weekly or monthly routines.

After coaching hundreds of clients, I noticed many are on overdrive, working long hours and making very little to no time for self-care. This experience inspired me to develop and share a simple and practical lifestyle program that empowers you to live a balanced life and revitalize your well-being. This lifestyle program focuses on four essential and interconnected areas of your well-being. These are described below and in more detail in the next pages.

THE FOUR ESSENTIALS TO BALANCED LIVING

- *Physical well-being:* Your body is your vessel. With it, you can experience life to the fullest. When you treat it well, you are helping it function at its most optimal level.
- *Mental well-being:* Managing and responding to life's stressors healthily can also positively impact the quality of your life.
- *Emotional well-being:* Allowing yourself to feel and tapping into the wisdom of your emotions are what breakthroughs are made of.
- *Spiritual well-being:* Within you lies a powerful force: your inner power. Your inner power and your connectedness to spirit—however you experience or define spirit—move you to live a meaningful, purposeful, and fulfilling life.

Taking care of your body, mind, heart, and spirit takes time. Carving out time is essential. You may need to reprioritize and put your well-being at the top of the list. To say "yes" to your well-being may mean saying "no" to other to-do's on your list. You may need to ask for help or hire help to allow yourself the time to balance yourself out. The more you do so, the more these basic healthy habits will become a big part of your way of life. Revitalizing your energy regularly will have you feeling good. When you feel good, you exude more confidence. This puts you in a better position to deal with the life circumstances that come your way.

Balanced living, combined with a solid connection to yourself and a clear vision, will help you stay on your path.

YOUR PHYSICAL WELL-BEING

Our physical well-being is affected by the care we give our body; our physical environment, whether our work environment or the home or city we live in; the company we keep; and how we manage our stressors. Let's take a moment to look at each one of these.

Body care

The care you give to your body is a reflection of the care you give to your mental, emotional, and spiritual well-being. There is an undeniable connection between our body, mind, heart, and spirit. To feel your best mentally, emotionally, and spiritually, take good care of your body, starting now. Here's how:

Physical exercise

Exercising thirty minutes most days, or four to five hours a week, will help release those feel-good endorphins and boost your metabolism. You can choose from a variety of exercises and mix it up. A combination of aerobic exercise, stretching. and strength training that suits you is what you are aiming for. And it need not be complicated. Keep your exercise routine simple and easily accessible so that you can do it anytime, anywhere. Here are some examples. You can go for a power walk in your neighborhood. You can bike with friends and family on the weekend. You can go out and buy yourself a mini-trampoline, tuck it under your bed, and pull it out in the morning to jump to your favorite music. You can purchase a Pilates and/or yoga DVD and work out from home. Join a gym. Take up dance exercise, such as a Zumba class. Or hire a personal trainer to get you started. The point is to make exercise fun and easy to get to. Having trouble committing? You can motivate yourself by committing to a 5K walk or run for a cause you are passionate about. Having an end in sight will motivate you to train in advance and get your body in shape. For those of you with a physical injury or other condition, it is important that you create an exercise routine that is appropriate for your bodily condition with your health-care professional.

Sleep

Let's talk sleep now. Getting eight hours of quality sleep a night is the ideal. Not only does it allow your body to heal itself, it's great for your skin. You know your clock better than anyone. Tune into it and aim to go to bed and wake up around the same times so that your body gets into a routine. Should you be having prolonged trouble sleeping, consult your doctor. Millions of people in North America suffer from sleep disorders. Untreated, sleep disorders can lead to other health complications.

Nutrition

As for nutrition, here are some general guidelines. The most important meal of your day is your breakfast. Starting out your morning with a healthy breakfast that includes a source of protein will help keep your blood sugar stable throughout the day. It's also essential to hydrate your body with adequate water:

eight to ten glasses of it on average, or 50 to 75 percent of your weight (in kilograms) in ounces of water. And, lastly, eat a balanced diet. Include five to nine servings of fruits and vegetables per day. Aim to have one fish meal a week: salmon, for instance, is a great source of omega-3 oil, which is good for your bones and memory. Reduce meats to about six ounces a day, and use lean meats and skinless poultry. Use healthy fats, such as olive oil. Add healthy snacks to your day, such as almonds or your own trail mix. Choose whole grains, such as steel-cut oats and whole-wheat breads. They are fiber rich and fill you up, regulating your appetite and aiding your digestion. For those who are sensitive to whole wheat or yeast, you can look for bread and pasta made from spelt or kamut. These are just as tasty. For those with lactose intolerance, go for lactose-free dairy. There are lactose-free cheeses and milk available in the market. Keep in mind that as we go from one stage of life to another, our dietary requirements may need to be tailored and supported with supplements. Discuss your nutritional requirements with your health-care professional.

Body treatments

Adequate and appropriate exercise, quality sleep, and healthy eating are the foundation to your body care. Body treatments, such as skin care, acupuncture, and massages, can be considered essential luxuries because of their relaxing qualities. They are the extra perks we give ourselves to feel and look good. And they need not break the bank. Skin care is a matter of choosing the right products to cleanse, hydrate, and moisturize your type of skin. There are many products out there to choose from, including natural, organic ones. Similarly, therapeutic massages and acupuncture delivered by a registered practitioner are covered by most health insurance plans. Lastly, you can always go for a home foot spa or an Epsom salt bath.

Image

When I think of image, I think of the clothes, jewelry, makeup, and hairstyle I wear. I also think of the presence I exude beyond the physical. That is, I ask myself, "What impact do I have on people, and what do they feel when they physically see me? How do I carry myself? What does my body language reveal? What does my voice reveal?" Presence comes from a state of being deep within you. For now, keep in mind that your emotional well-being and how you see yourself has a direct impact on your physical image. So what you wear and your hairstyle are a reflection of your inner state.

Know and believe in who you are, your values, and your life aspirations when deciding what to wear and how to carry yourself. This can be challenging to do, particularly for women, where much emphasis is placed on having a youthful sexy look. We are bombarded with advertisements for an array of beauty products to help keep us young. Now I'm not suggesting that looking and feeling your best must rule out any of these products. What I am suggesting is for you to base your choices on using products you believe are right for you because *you* think so, not because someone else thinks so. The reality is that we are all aging. We need to accept it and allow nature to take its course. We can look and feel our best at every stage of life.

Environment

Where we live, work, and play make a difference to our physical well-being. Ever notice how some colors bring you to life and others calm you? Well, that's your environment at work. Ever notice how a messy and unclean home or office impacts your physical state? How about the air quality or noise level in your city? What about the people you socialize with or work with? How do they affect your physical state? The point here is that we are connected to everyone and everything around us. Noticing your environment and its impact on you can reveal what is supporting your physical well-being and what is not. Once you notice this, you can choose to either accept or transform your environments.

Physical well-being is about sticking to your maintenance plan. Once you do, your body will soon choose healthier options naturally.

EXERCISE: PHYSICAL CARE

1. What areas of your physical well-being need more attention? Circle each item below that you would like to improve.
   a. Physical exercise
   b. Sleep
   c. Nutrition
   d. Body treatments
      i. Therapeutic massages
      ii. Acupuncture
      iii. Skin care
      iv. Other
   e. Image
      i. Hair
      ii. Makeup (if applicable)
      iii. Wardrobe
      iv. Accessories
      v. Body language/posture
   f. Physical environment
      i. Organization
      ii. Décor
      iii. Cleanliness
      iv. Air quality
      v. Noise level
      vi. People in your space
      vii. Other

2. How is your career impacting your physical well-being?

3. How are your finances impacting your physical well-being?

4. What else is getting in the way of your physical well-being?

Physical movement plan

Form of movement	Times/week	Duration	Buddy
Power walk			
Run			
Cycling			
Yoga/ stretching			
Strength training			
Pilates			
Other			

Choose the physical movements you enjoy and want to include in your plan. You can also add your own tailored activities. Remember to consult your health-care practitioner(s) to choose exercises that are right for your physical condition.

Sleep plan

I commit to sleeping _____ hours a day.

You know the amount of sleep you need that has you feeling good. Having trouble sleeping? Speak with your health-care practitioner(s).

Nutrition plan

Sources of nutrition	Amount per day
Proteins • Fish • Poultry • Other lean meats	
Fruits	
Beans and legumes	
Vegetables	
Whole grains • Pasta • Cereals • Breads • Snacks	
Water	
Other	

Remember, aim for five to nine servings of fruits and vegetables. Each serving is half a cup. On average, 50 to 75 percent of your weight (in kilograms) is your daily water intake requirement (in ounces). Include fiber-rich foods, such as fruits, beans, legumes, and whole grains. Your required fiber intake depends on your gender and age. As you go from one stage of life to another, you may discover that you need dietary supplements, including vitamins such as B, C, and D, and minerals such as magnesium and iron. Discuss your nutritional requirements with your health-care practitioner(s). Your body is an intelligent vessel that is the home of your beautiful spirit. Start taking care of your body today.

YOUR MENTAL WELL-BEING

Depression is among the leading causes of disability worldwide. Stress plays a major role.

What is stress, and where does it come from?

Being exposed to stressors is a natural part of life. We face life difficulties and pressures throughout our lifetime, with work and financial pressures being the most widespread, and family, health, and relationship issues coming in at a close second.

How we perceive these stressors and the way we deal with them determines whether or not we will experience stress, which is a physiological, psychological, and/or social reaction. The more effective our coping strategies are, the less likely we will make ourselves sick in body, mind, and spirit. Learning coping skills and applying them regularly will help prevent the cumulative effects of stress.

Some signs of stress or burnout

- Fatigue or sleeplessness
- Ongoing sadness
- Irritability and/or lashing out
- Panic attacks
- Withdrawal and/or communication breakdown
- Lack of focus and concentration
- Other noticeable change in appearance, behavior, and/or performance

Central to stress is the desire to control all aspects of our life. The reality is that some situations are beyond our control, and the only thing we can control is our self. Seeing change as an integral part of our life, instead of seeing it as a threat, puts us in a better position to cope effectively with stressors.

Career, money, and happiness

We all need to survive: we need to pay for the home we sleep in, the food we eat, the clothes we wear, etc. So how does one create balance and fulfillment when one is in "making money" mode? Well, some people choose to create balance and fulfillment outside of work. Their work means less to them than providing for their family, for example. Some people are in a "making money" job with little to no inherent satisfaction solely for the sake of pursuing another dream, such as actors who wait on tables to make ends meet while they pursue their dream acting role. Others choose to change their lifestyle so that they can love their work and their life, such as entrepreneurs who downsize and sell their car to invest in their new endeavor.

After a decade of unhappiness, I approached my employer at the time and asked for help mapping out my career path. And I got it. After three months of intense career coaching and assessments, I began to solidify my career direction. I knew what parts of my jobs I had enjoyed up until that point, and those parts pointed to a different career. I started the career transition gradually by taking another position within the company I worked at. After a couple of years, I gained the confidence and conviction it took to boldly step into entrepreneurship. I was financially, mentally, and emotionally ready to make the lifestyle changes necessary to make it happen. I chose to make less and spend less, and invest some of my savings and funds from a government grant I qualified for to start a business that reflects who I am. What I'm realizing as I continue to grow my business is that the income potential is immense. That being said, entrepreneurship comes with its own set of challenges. You have to have an entrepreneurial spirit and an ability to surf the waves of entrepreneurship. Like an ocean, entrepreneurship can be stormy, while at other times calm and serene.

Every person is unique. What is right for one person may not be right for another. For every choice, there is a consequence. That is, some values take priority while others take the backseat. Deciding which values take priority and which take the backseat is a very personal decision. As time passes, values and priorities may change. It's important to notice when a choice that once felt right and fulfilling no longer feels so. The key is to know what matters to you the most at any time, and plan accordingly.

Money makes the world go 'round—or does it?

Much emphasis is placed on money in most places around the world. Any given government's success is largely measured by its economic growth. Money has become central to our lives. Yet results from various studies measuring people's happiness based on income have been conflicting. Some longitudinal studies show that over the last fifty years, people's happiness in prosperous nations hardly changes when their income changes. In other words, the growth in economic output over the last fifty years has not translated into more happiness.[5] There seems to be something deeper going on in the hearts and minds of these people.

This may explain why some countries are beginning to re-examine and change the way they measure their progress. Several countries are considering following Bhutan's lead in using "Gross National Happiness" to measure their progress, alongside the traditional yardstick of "Gross National Product." What this means is that they'll be monitoring the effectiveness of their governance, socioeconomic development, environmental protection, and preservation of culture.[6]   These are all interconnected. How we make money, how much we make relative to our cost of living, how we use it, who is given the opportunity to make and have money, and who is given the training, education, and government support to make and have money all play a part in our world's progress. Many organizations around the world are increasingly supporting and empowering women around the world to get an education and start a business. Approximately 50 percent of our world's population is made up of women, many of whom historically have been deprived of an education. What has become clear in recent years is that when a woman is supported and empowered to get an education and start a business, she not only transforms herself, she transforms her community.

Certainly, there is more to happiness than making and having money. That being said, there is a certain amount of money people need to meet their basic needs at a minimum. While this amount varies from one part of the world to another, one thing remains constant: the more people meet their basic needs, the more people will have the capacity to develop into their full potential. The more people develop into their full potential, the more our world will flourish.

The reality is that billions of people in our world are living in poverty. Most of this poverty is found in Africa and Indo-Asia. And in the West, income disparities are growing. The cost of living is increasing while incomes are remaining stagnant. Some of my friends are working twelve-hour days to keep up, while raising children. Some are choosing to downsize, because the stress of keeping up is having adverse effects on their health, performance, quality of life, and time with their family. They are choosing to sell the second car and house in the country. This reality is calling us to re-examine how we lead our work and life, and how we can contribute to make a difference.

Being an entrepreneur has allowed me to fully utilize my strengths, develop in very exciting ways, express myself, and ask myself some tough questions, such as "How much money do I really need? What will I do with more money than I need?" Growing up, I had the privilege of spending my summers in a small home on a Greek island that had no electricity until the late seventies. We used well water for cleaning and showering. We rationed our fresh food, as there was only so much we could bring in from Athens and buy from the locals. This island had one road and a handful of cars. The sun, the ocean, and clean air enveloped us. Yes, I was young and carefree. Yes, I was there for only a few months a year. I did, however, get a taste of a basic, simple, yet very happy life. This experience provided me with another perspective, a perspective that enabled me to adjust my lifestyle and downsize with ease so that I could invest in my business. I knew I could be happy just the same. At the same time, envisioning what I'd do with more money has been a challenge. After some contemplation and exploration, I have a clearer picture now. Particularly after writing this book, it has become clear to me that I want to help people around the world get their basic needs met so that they can focus on developing their full potential. The better my business performs, the more I intend to give back. My success can be the world's success.

While being wealthy does not necessarily add up to being happy, being poor comes with its own set of problems, such as hunger; disease; and limited access to shelter, education, and health care—a vicious cycle. Striking a balance is essential. Will using Gross National Happiness as a measure of our progress help us prosper? We'll have to see. For now, striking a balance in our own life is what we can focus on.

Stress mastery modalities

With financial and work pressures being the most prevalent daily life stressors, learning to cope can help you perform well under these pressures and preserve your health. Below are some stress-mastery modalities you can use on a regular basis to maintain your overall well-being and a healthy head-heart dialogue.

- *Deep breathing techniques:* Take at least three deep breaths, inhaling through your nose on the count of 4 and exhaling through your nose on the count of 4. When you inhale, feel your diaphragm expanding, like a balloon being inflated. When you exhale, feel your diaphragm contracting, sinking back into your body. Do this several times throughout the day. You'll feel more relaxed.

- *Silent meditation:* Nurture your mind by meditating daily for at least five minutes. That means sitting in silence and simply being with yourself, focusing on the sound of your breathing and allowing all thoughts to rise and leave your mind. You can do this anywhere, such as on the subway to work. This may seem unproductive to you. The reality is that it is very productive in a way that is invisible to the eye. What this does is clear the space in your mind. With a clutter-free mind, you can see a situation in new ways, come up with new ideas, enjoy the calmness that comes with meditation, and make empowering choices from this place.

- *Walking meditation:* Place your focus on your surroundings, your body movement, or your breath. Placing your attention on the present moment will help relieve tension.

- *Body scanning:* Lie down on a comfortable mat on the floor. Relax one body part at a time, starting from your feet and moving up to the top of your head. Notice where you are holding the tension. Imagine the tension leaving your body.

- *Yoga:* You can also practice mindful meditation while placing your attention on your breath and yoga poses. The idea is to listen to your body, thoughts, and feelings without judging yourself. Yoga can help release the negativity trapped in your mind and body. For all you fellows out there who think you must be able to touch your toes to do yoga, I have news for you, too. Yoga is not about competition or pushing yourself to nail a pose. Yoga is about accepting yourself and raising your awareness. All you have to do is listen to and trust yourself.

- *Vision work:* Manage your inner mocker by focusing on your vision. Listen to guided visualizations, journal about your vision, and/or create a vision board.
- *Affirmations:* Declutter your mind by replacing old self-limiting beliefs with affirmations you genuinely believe and feel good repeating.
- *Body care:* Release tension through body work, such as shiatsu massage therapy or acupuncture.

Monthly body treatments are part of my wellness program. I reintroduced shiatsu massage therapy and the occasional acupuncture session on a monthly basis, because the consistency allows me to stay centered and feel better. The monthly body treatments remind me what it feels like to be in total equilibrium. This feeling of equilibrium in my body is what sets me up for a positive and productive day.

Body work such as acupuncture and shiatsu massage helps restore vital energy by releasing subconscious emotional blocks trapped in our body tissue. Releasing emotional blocks through body work creates room for your best, authentic, loving self to step into its renewed life. For one thing, you become aware of what has been holding you back. You feel it oozing out of you. As it is released from you physically, you also let go of your attachment to it. It no longer lives inside of you. Whatever it is no longer controls you. Space is created for a renewed life, a life full of empowering choices. Speak to your health-care practitioner about the benefits of regular body work.

Also, be sure your diet includes foods and supplements that reduce the release of stress hormones, such as cortisol. Your health-care practitioner can guide you.

- *Talking it out:* Hire a coach or counselor, or open up to family and friends.
- *Laughter:* When you laugh, your body releases feel-good hormones.

    On my way home the other night, I found myself amused by the sound of a senior's hearty laughter on the bus. A small smile came across my face the first time I heard his laughter. He laughed again a little longer. This time I tried to contain myself, as I was sitting alone in my seat. He laughed again even longer. At this point, many of us looked back to see who this infectious laughter was coming out of. We turned back to our original positions with wide smiles on our faces and silently laughed along with him. Even our eyes were smiling to one another. At that moment, I remembered what a gift it is to share our laughter. This senior man was by himself, too. It didn't matter. The sound of his laughter connected us all, regardless of our abilities, gender, race, age, and so on. Laughter is a boost to your well-being, as "feel-good" hormones get released in your body. So remember to add laughter to your day!

- *Joyful activities:* Spend time doing what you find joyful, such as a hobby or time with your family, and be sure to surround yourself with positive and supportive people.

- *Pet your furry pet friend:* Notice your heart opening up and the accompanying thoughts. This is why animal therapy is a growing field. Nursing homes are increasingly integrating pet sessions. Pets improve the quality of life and health of their owners/companions. They truly are a gift on earth.

EXERCISE: STRESS MANAGEMENT

1. List your life stressors.

2. Which of these life stressors are you giving more energy to than you need to?

3. Which of these do you want to deal with more healthily?

4. What can you do to deal with your life stressors more healthily?

YOUR EMOTIONAL WELL-BEING

Emotional well-being is about accepting and feeling your emotions. All of them. All too often, we experience conflicting emotions, or we avoid the so-called negative ones. When we reject our feelings, we reject ourselves. And the more we avoid certain feelings, the more they remain. When we accept and feel our emotions, we make room for personal growth and self-love.

Feeling your emotions

You feel your emotions in your body. Unlike your mind, which compares, evaluates, and judges based on the past or the future, your body is always in the moment, experiencing what is through your emotions. We experience both positive and negative emotions. After all, life is dualistic.

Light emotions	Heavy emotions
Fearlessness/Calmness	Fear/Panic/Anxiety/Nervousness
Empowerment/Forgiveness/ Admiration	Anger/Rage/Contempt/ Powerlessness
Satisfaction/Love/Pride	Frustration/Lust/Humiliation
Abundance/Independence	Hunger/Neediness
Worthiness/Assertiveness/ Meaningfulness	Worthlessness/Intimidation/ Emptiness
Connectedness/Contentment/ Happiness	Loneliness/Longing/Sadness
Confidence/Groundedness/ Connectedness	Doubt/Airiness/Disconnectedness
Self-Acceptance	Self-Criticism
Integration/Hope/Selflessness/ Fulfillment	Isolation/Despair/Selfishness/ Unfulfillment

Resisting the heavy feelings creates pain in your body. That being said, there could be a certain amount of momentary pain when experiencing heavy feelings. This pain is intensified when you resist and suppress your heavy feelings. The beauty is that when you allow your heavy feelings to coexist with you (rather than take you over), you give them the space to move through you, like a visitor. Your heavy feelings want you to notice them, because behind them lies your potential, your transformation. Take any heavy feeling above, and notice how it can be transformed into a light one. Your heavy feelings are clues for you in solving your own mystery.

> In a coaching program I deliver yearly, a small group of like-minded women dared to explore the emotions they resisted the most. Courageously, each one shared what was behind the resistance. As we dug deeper, the wisdom in their emotions came through, and their unexpressed longing was revealed. To get to their joyful vision, we befriended their painful emotions. What a release! Clearing our emotions daily in this way helps create the space for authentic positivity, the kind you truly feel, embody, and share with others.

Letting go and letting love in

Just like our heavy feelings, experiencing loss or significant change is also a normal part of life. When we experience any kind of loss or transition, we will go through certain emotional stages. You may have heard of the five stages of grief, introduced by Elisabeth Kübler-Ross: denial, anger, bargaining, depression, and acceptance.

> Looking back, I did go through all those after my divorce, but not exactly in that order. What I also recognized years after my divorce and into the dating scene was that I was repeating a pattern! I was getting hooked on drama. My cousin pointed this out to me one day, as I sat on her couch going on and on about stuff. That was a

pivotal moment for me. She mirrored back to me exactly what I needed to admit to myself, accept about myself, and allow myself to release so that I could let in more love into my life. That is exactly what I have done since. I have let love in, starting with love for myself. I have learned to know and love myself. Now I catch myself and quickly let go of unnecessary drama.

When we know and love ourselves unconditionally, we can create a life we love that is full of love, no matter what circumstances and emotional stages we need to process. Our entire journey is absolutely beautiful, designed to help us grow in ways we never imagined.

Responding to your emotions

Over time, you will begin to notice your emotional patterns. Behind your emotional patterns lies a deep inner wisdom, a wisdom that, once harnessed, will help you release old, limiting beliefs and help you choose your course of action or inaction powerfully.

Emotional wisdom is available to all. That is, when you allow yourself to listen to what your emotions are revealing about yourself and your circumstances, you stand a chance to break through and gain empowering insights. Some emotions are scarier than others. Some mask deep-rooted pain, anger, or fear. I've been there and been through it.

Taking the time to notice your emotional patterns over time is a wise investment in your personal development. Journal your emotions for a week, and notice what shows up. Do you allow yourself to experience your emotions? Or do you resist them? Be your own witness. Every emotion, light or dark, is a guidepost.

To have a responsible emotional experience, here is a framework you can apply in your daily life:

- Experience your feelings: notice what is showing up. Be your own witness. You need not react or act at this point (unless you are in a life-threatening situation).
- Process your feelings: notice their impact on you and others.
  - ✓ Start an emotional journal.
  - ✓ Meditate.
  - ✓ Get curious and explore your emotions.
  - ✓ Trust yourself.
  - ✓ Talk about your feelings with a friend or family member you trust.
  - ✓ Celebrate your light, or those moments where all is well.
- Understand your feelings: notice what triggers them and what they are revealing to you.
  - ✓ Understand your darkness and how it is directing you to wholeness.
  - ✓ Embrace your light and how it can assist you into living out your full potential.
  - ✓ What do you really want?
- Manage your feelings: choose how best to deal with the circumstances giving rise to your feelings in a way that honors you and your relationships with others.

Relationships and your emotions

Dealing with your emotions in a healthy way will help you deal with others' emotions in a healthy way as well. The better you get at dealing with your emotions, the better you will be with others'. Your ability to empathize is pivotal to developing healthy relationships with others, be they friends, family, work colleagues, or your community at large. You can apply a similar framework, as noted above, when dealing with others' emotions. Applying this framework will also help you remain objective, rather than reacting to others' emotions or taking others' emotions personally.

That being said, we usually attract people and circumstances that reflect our own emotional state of being. And, at an unconscious level, we may project suppressed feelings from past events onto other persons or events. However, these persons or events are not the cause of our feelings; they are the triggers. We are ultimately responsible. The world around us is indeed our mirror. Handling the feelings that come with our projections, as in above framework, is essential so as to not re-suppress our feelings.

Increasing positivity in your relationships

Did you know that stable marriages have a 5 to 1 ratio of positive to negative interactions?[7]

Let's assume, then, that this ratio applies to other relationships. Either increasing positivity or reducing negativity will be beneficial. Increasing positivity can be as simple as using humor, laughter, a smile, affection, respectful dialoguing, etc.

When you can experience, process, understand, and manage your emotions as described in the framework above, you'll be able to increase positivity and reduce negativity in your relationships all the more easily.

Emotional freedom and resilience radiates confidence and magnetism.

EXERCISE: EMOTIONAL WISDOM

1. Which emotions do you experience more often?

2. Which emotions do you resist more often?

3. What would happen if you allowed yourself to feel your emotions?

4. Where in your body do you experience these different emotions? Describe.

5. What are your emotions trying to tell you?

6. What is currently supporting your emotional well-being?

7. What else would nurture your emotional well-being?

8. How are your emotions impacting your relationships?

9. What can you do to increase positivity in your relationships?

YOUR SPIRITUAL WELL-BEING

Your spiritual well-being is an essential part of your intellectual, emotional, and physical health. Ever notice how in times of crisis your faith in yourself, others, and a higher power are revealed? Deep within you is this incredible power to transform your life so that your full potential can express itself. Your innate power is what enables you to discover the essence of your being, your deepest values, and your purpose.

I have learned to accept that some of the things that happened in my life are a mystery and have no logical or rational explanation, at least at this time. These experiences have led me to believe that there is indeed a sixth sense and that we are more than physical. We are spirit. While working with my shiatsu therapist, I discovered that I can sense people's energy. I could sense my shiatsu therapist's energy. Early into our work, I had had a strong feeling he was not well. My feeling was so strong that I had addressed this with him, which was unusual for me then. He explained that everything was fine, and that he was on top of it and seeking medical attention. I let it go. Months after that he got curious and asked me, "Who are you?" and I replied softly, "I am spiritual." He wanted to know what I meant. I whispered, "I sense things," and stopped. I had such a hard time sharing this part of myself. Much of our society denies this aspect of our being because of the widespread belief that if we can't perceive it without our five senses, it isn't real. He, on the other hand, immediately acknowledged and related to what I was talking about. He was a gifted man, no doubt; a man who, in a twist of fate, validated my own divine gifts. Knowing him helped me open up to the nonphysical world within and around us. Although he has crossed over, his essence will always live in my heart.

Intuition

Intuition is a sense of knowing that does not depend on a logical explanation. Some people call it a "gut feeling." Others call it a "psychic phenomenon." Whatever we call it, it exists, and we can all tap into this realm of knowing. On its own, this knowing may not be 100 percent correct, though. Consider it another form of communication that can be misinterpreted.

Quantum physicists are still trying to prove that a type of energy, or what they call *quantum fluctuations*, exists in the "empty space" within and around us that is connected and informs us. Don't let that stop you. Coaches use their intuition all the time when coaching. We feel and sense what is in the space between the coach and the client, and communicate this to our clients. We tap into our intuition to help clients tap into theirs. Clients have a chance to add to this, correct it, and build from there. There is no loss in putting your intuition out there. How you communicate it is the key. Being intuitive is not about being right; it's about being of service to others, to your relationships, and to yourself. In combination with our heart and mind, intuition can be a very empowering force in our lives and workplaces.

Intuition feeds our heart, which feeds our mind.

Spiritual practices that can nurture your innate power

- Meditation
- Yoga
- Prayer
- Contemplation
- Mandala healing art

Benefits of spiritual practice

The benefits of spiritual practice are many. Spiritual practice enables you to witness your life with clarity, integrity, and nonattachment. Your values and what matters most to you become more obvious to you. With clarity, finding your purpose and experiencing more meaning in your life is a natural progression. As you gain this clarity, you begin to connect with others from a richer and deeper place within you, because your heart, mind, and spirit are one.

Spiritual practice also cultivates more self-acceptance and peace within you. Studies have shown that when a small group of people come together to meditate and achieve peace within themselves, this peace is reflected in their surroundings.[8] Imagine what could be possible.

With consistent spiritual practice, you can become a whole leader, enriching your work, life, and relationships, as you become ever more present in the moment and connected to your core self.

EXERCISE: SPIRITUAL WISDOM

1. Do you believe in the concept of a higher power? Please describe the most empowering aspects of your spirituality.

2. If you believe in the concept of a higher power, how do you connect with it?

3. What is most meaningful in your life?

4. What is your purpose in life? How will you make a difference?

5. How do you nurture your spiritual well-being? Circle each that applies.
   a. Meditation
   b. Yoga
   c. Prayer
   d. Contemplation
   e. Other (describe)

6. What is getting in the way of your spiritual well-being?

7. What else can you do to nurture your spiritual well-being?

PART IV

Your LITE in Action

I step out beyond the known to claim
the riches of my true potential.

Alan Cohen

CHAPTER SEVEN

Your Path: Moving from Here to There

Our deepest yearning is to live a purposeful life. Our purpose is a reflection of who we are at the core, our gifts, and the impact we want and know we can have on the world. Some people discover it at a very early age. I have had the honor of meeting some amazing world athletes and champions during my career. These athletes knew from a young age who they wanted to be one day and what they wanted to do with their life. Today, these champions use their profile to make a difference. They go on to be ambassadors of good causes, write books, speak, and spread empowering messages. Similarly, we see starving actors and singers go through painstaking journeys to fame; with that fame, they mobilize millions of people through their creativity, empowering messages, and charity contributions. Others awaken during a midlife crisis and realize there must be more to life.

However it happens for you, or anyone else, is part of the magic. Along your path, wherever you are on it, lie your gifts. Their sparkle and shine will reflect back who you are. Your part is to take the time to notice, self-reflect, and open up to the possibilities; to believe that you have something unique to offer to our world and can make a difference.

Every difference, big or small, matters. In most cases, the difference we make is immeasurable and intangible. When you are seen, heard, and experienced for who you are, you are having a ripple effect on the people you know, and they on the people they know, and so on. In other words, when you are being your authentic self and sharing your gifts with loving intention, you will make a positive difference; you simply may never know the full extent of the difference you make. This may come to you as a relief. After all, it can be overwhelming to think about all the world issues that need to be addressed. The perfectionist in you may decide to avoid the whole journey because it feels too big a task.

Remember this: you are not alone, and you alone are not expected to solve all the world's problems. All you can do is be seen, heard, and experienced for who you are. When you do this, you are encouraging and empowering others to do the same. There is joy and fulfillment to experience throughout your entire journey.

KEY INGREDIENTS TO STAY THE COURSE

- *Courage:* To take responsibility for yourself and your life.
- *Clarity:* Discovering who you are meant to be and what you are meant to do.
- *Commitment:* To stick it out during the highs and lows of your journey.

- *Consistency:* To keep the momentum of your personal growth going.
- *Conviction:* To persevere no matter what, because it's who you are.

You've got the courage. You are already taking responsibility for yourself and your life as you work through this book. To stay the course, it's important to do the next exercise. This next exercise will help you put it all together and identify your next action steps. Step into action, bringing all the key ingredients above into it. At the same time, go with the flow, pay attention to how you feel, listen to your inner wisdom, and adjust your steps as you move forward.

There have been times when I have asked myself, "Why am I doing what I'm doing? Will it really make a difference in the grand scheme of things? How big of a difference am I really making?" By asking myself these questions, I realized that I'd do it anyhow, because I love and enjoy what I'm doing. I am being me doing what I do. And the difference I make with even just one person means the world to me.

Remember, this is about you being your full potential and sharing your strengths, passions, and innate gifts. That alone will make a difference. There is joy to be had in the process of becoming and sharing all that you are!

Be your LITE, and you shall shine LITE on others.

EXERCISE: PUTTING IT TOGETHER AND TAKING ACTION

What do you want more of in each area of your life? Go back to the exercises throughout the book, and pull out what you value most and want more of in your life. Then write down some specific action steps you can take to honor your values and create the life you want. Set some timelines, and commit to following through on your action steps.

Area of your life	Want/ need	Goal(s)	Action steps	Timeline
Self-esteem				
Leadership				
Intellect				
Teamwork				
Expression				
Physical well-being				
Mental well-being				
Emotional well-being				
Spiritual well-being				

CONCLUSION

Gratitude

Gratitude

Everything in this universe is happening by brilliant design to awaken our drive to make this a better world. Were it not for darkness, we would not know light. This is the world we live in, one of duality. Whatever it is that enrages you, be it the injustice in some parts of the world or the inequalities in your community, your experience of this is what awakens your drive to make a positive difference. Some experiences touch the very core of our soul. Cherish these experiences, for they are your guiding light. Allow yourself to be with whatever emotions arise, and listen to their wisdom. Your emotions can be transformed into positive action and change.

You may be asking, "Why make this a better world?" The answer I have come up with is to preserve life on earth. Whether you are single and childless, or a parent or grandparent, one thing we all have in common is our natural instinct to evolve and preserve life. These very natural instincts are what keep us from self-destruction. Think about how the earth naturally self-regulates and protects us with its magnetic field. Were it not for the earth's core producing the earth's magnetic field, our earth would be in danger. We are no different than our earth. We, like the earth, are designed to preserve life, so long as we are alive and well. By allowing our core to radiate our essence, we contribute to our humanity's well-being.

Now you may be asking, "Why preserve life?" So many world problems seem out of control: weather anomalies, famines, diseases, limited resources, greed, corruption, wars, sex and drug trafficking, etc. While these are serious issues to consider, they are also what drive us to advance our world. This drive comes from a deep gratitude for what is beautiful about life on earth: love, peace, joy, nature, art, culture, diversity, relationships with all their ups and downs, connectedness, community, personal growth, etc.

How you live your life makes a difference to others and our planet. Respecting ourselves, each other, our humanity, and our planet is the gateway to conscious living. When we live consciously, we awaken others to do the same, one by one. This is within our control.

THINGS TO REMEMBER

1. Look inside yourself for happiness.
2. Know and love your core self unconditionally.
3. Let your essence and innate gifts inspire your purposeful vision.
4. Lead with your whole heart and mind.
5. Communication is the bridge between your heart and mind, and you and the world around you.
6. Master your mind.

7. Sustain unity by focusing on your vision and team strengths.
8. Let the world see, hear, and experience you for who you are.
9. Take care of your body, mind, heart, and spirit.
10. You can get from here to there with courage, clarity, commitment, and conviction.
11. We live in a world of duality that is brilliantly assisting us to be whole again.

This brings us to the end of this book, and the beginning of infinite possibilities for your life. Take some time now to visualize and write down what is possible for your whole life.

You are a circle of LITE! Imagine a world of LITE!

ENDNOTES

[1] Glenn R. Schiraldi, Ph.D., *The Self-Esteem Workbook* (Oakland: New Harbinger, 2001), p. 33.

[2] Joseph Chilton Pearce, *The Biology of Transcendence* (Rochester: Park Street Press, 2004), pp. 4, 23, and 64.

[3] Joseph Murphy, *The Power of Your Subconscious Mind* (New York: Prentice Hall Press, 2008), pp. 16–17..

[4] David Richo, *When the Past Is Present* (Boston: Shambhala, 2008), p. 62.

[5] Derek Bok, *The Politics of Happiness* (Princeton: Princeton University Press, 2010), p. 11.

[6] Derek Bok, *The Politics of Happiness* (Princeton: Princeton University Press, 2010), pp. 1–2

[7] John M. Gottman, *The Marriage Clinic: A Scientifically-Based Marital Therapy* (New York: Norton, 1999), p. 88.

[8] Gregg Braden, *The Divine Matrix* (Carlsbad: Hay House, 2007), p. 116.

REFERENCES

Atwood, Janet Bray and Chris. *The Passion Test.* New York: Plume, 2008.

Benstead, Deborah and Storm Constantine. *The Inward Revolution.* London: Warner Books, 1998.

Chopra, Deepak, Debbie Ford, and Marianne Williamson. *The Shadow Effect.* New York: Harper One, 2010.

Gawain, Shakti. *The Path of Transformation.* Novato, CA: Nataraj, 2000.

Halpern, Belle Linda and Kathy Lubar, *Leadership Presence.* New York: Gotham Books, 2003.

Hanson, Rick and Richard Mendius. *Buddha's Brain.* Oakland: New Harbinger, 2009.

Hicks, Esther and Jerry. *The Law of Attraction.* Carlsbad: Hay House, 2007.

Kabat-Zinn, Jon. *Full Catastrophe Living.* New York: Delta, 2009.

Kelley, Tim. *True Purpose.* Berkeley: Transcendent Solutions Press, 2009.

Pearce, Joseph Chilton. *The Biology of Transcendence*. Rochester: Park Street Press, 2004.

Rosenberg, Marshall B. *Nonviolent Communication*. Encinitas: Puddle Dancer Press, 2003.

Ruskan, John. *Emotional Clearing*. New York: Broadway Books, 2000.

Schiraldi, Glenn R. *The Self-Esteem Workbook*. Oakland: New Harbinger, 2001.

Simon, David. *Free to Love, Free to Heal*. Carlsbad: Chopra Center Press, 2009.

Tolle, Eckhart. *A New Earth*. New York: Plume, 2006.

Tolle, Eckhart. *The Power of Now*. Novato, CA: New World Library, 2004.

ACKNOWLEDGEMENTS

Writing this book has reminded me of the blessings in every experience and encounter I've had. Each step I took in life has helped me shape this book. So, really, I want to acknowledge everyone and everything that have played a part in my life. I would like to express special thanks to the following people and organizations:

- My family: it's big and Greek and includes our pets. Thank you for loving me as I am—all of me—and cheering me on. Our family has been and continues to be a great learning ground for unconditional love. We have laughed, cried, argued, forgiven, made-up, loved, and huddled. We've explored every range of emotion and will continue to, I'm sure. Through it all, we've strengthened our relationships.
- My long-time and close friends (you know who you are), for always listening and sharing your own wise insights.
- Brendon Burchard, co-founder of the Experts Industry Association, and my publisher, Morgan James Publishing, for their innovation and expertise. You have made this book possible.

- You, the readers of this book, you are leaders who make a difference. Without you, the impact of this book would go unnoticed.
- The teachers, coaches, authors, and speakers who have inspired and encouraged me to carry on and express my own full potential.
- The coaching organizations that have certified me and provided me with the tools that allow me to offer the holistic coaching services that I do. They are the Coaches Training Institute, Team Coaching International™, and The Leadership Circle®.
- The universe, for its mysterious ways.

Thank you all!

MEET THE AUTHOR

Helen Roditis, B. Comm., CA, ACC
Leadership Coach and Founder of essence coaching
www.essencecoaching.ca

Living well and working well are what Helen stands for. Such balance is essential in engaging talent, developing their full potential, and turning vision into reality. As an Associate Certified Coach, Helen has helped hundreds of individuals, business leaders, and organizational teams transform their life, career, and workplace. She does this by raising their self-awareness, cultivating their strengths, and integrating wellness into her coaching programs. With over twenty years of diverse experience in corporate finance, marketing, and consulting, Helen can see 360 degrees when working with her clients. Her strong business acumen, integrity, and warm personality build immediate trust with her clients and empower her coaching relationships. She also shares her knowledge and experience through her writing. Her articles "Empower Your People and Reap the Rewards" and "Proactively Managing Employee Stress" have been published in Canadian business magazines. Passionate about helping professionals and business teams develop their full potential, Helen is busy these days writing, speaking, and delivering her coaching programs. You may contact Helen by telephone at 416-322-3623, or by e-mail at hroditis@essencecoaching.ca.

ABOUT ESSENCE COACHING

Holistic coaching solutions that help boost performance inside and outside the workplace are what make working with essence coaching so effective. Coaching services such as career, work/life balance, stress management, leadership, and team development are available in one-on-one or group sessions. These services are all interconnected. Essentially, essence coaching facilitates positive change in professionals' lives, careers, and work environment by taking a big-picture approach.

What is coaching?

Coaching is an empowering, thought-provoking, and creative process that inspires clients to maximize their personal and professional potential. The coaching process is meant to help clients achieve extraordinary results, based on goals set by the individual or team. The focus is on the skills and actions needed to successfully produce their personally relevant results (as defined by the International Coach Federation).

Coaching is not therapy, nor is it advice giving. This is what makes coaching so empowering. You are viewed as naturally creative, resourceful, and whole. Your coach's role is to listen and bring out the answers that lie within you.

Who hires essence coaching?

- Professionals and entrepreneurs yearning for more clarity, meaning, balance, and opportunity for growth in their work and life.
- Progressive organizations/teams who want to retain their talent, support their development, and consequently turn their vision into reality.

UPCOMING EVENTS

FREE INTRODUCTORY WEBINAR: LITE UP YOUR WORK AND LIFE!

- You will be introduced to the Circle of LITE coaching model designed by Helen Roditis, the founder of essence coaching. The Circle of LITE coaching model is intended to help you develop and express your full potential at work and in your life, one step at a time.
- This introductory webinar is held two times a year at minimum, typically in the spring and fall.
- To find out more and register, go to: www.circleoflite.com.
- Additional bonuses: FREE resources are available at www. essencecoaching.ca.

COACHING PROGRAM: CIRCLE OF LITE

This is an eight-week online group coaching program. This program comes with the option of adding one-on-one coaching, space permitting. We'll be spending approximately two weekly 90-minute webinar sessions on each of the parts below. This program is delivered two times a year at minimum, in the spring and fall.

PART I: Know & Love Your Core Self

PART II: LITE Up Your Work

PART III: LITE Up Your Life

PART IV: Your Full Potential in Action

To find out more and register, go to: www.circleoflite.com.

CPSIA information can be obtained at www.ICGtesting.com
Printed in the USA
LVOW130709180912

299182LV00005B/4/P